Contemporary Machine-Embroidered Accessories

Transform Everyday Accessories into Designer Originals

Eileen Roche

©2007 Eileen Roche

Published by

kp **krause publications**
An Imprint of F+W Publications

700 East State Street • Iola, WI 54990-0001
715-445-2214 • 888-457-2873
www.krausebooks.com

Our toll-free number to place an order or obtain
a free catalog is (800) 258-0929.

The following registered trademark terms and companies appear in this publication:
UltraSuede, Magna-Hoop, Pellon, ShirTailor, Floriani Stitch N Shape, Fasturn, Res-Q Tape, Sulky Totally Stable, Buzz Tools, Buzz Edit, Stitch Editor, Husqvarna Viking, Bernina Editor, PE-Design, Brother, Generations, Origins, Explorations, OESD, Designer's Gallery Studio, Baby Lock, Pfaff Creative Stitch Editor, Digitizer 10000, Janome, Professional Sew Ware, Singer, Amazing Designs, Edit N Stitch, X-ACTO, EmbroideryArts, Romanesque, Designs in Machine Embroidery, Angle Finder, Chalk-O-Liner, Microsoft Windows, Sharpie, Schmetz, Fiskars.

Library of Congress Control Number: 2006935754

ISBN-13: 978-0-89689-491-4
ISBN-10: 0-89689-491-6

Edited by Andy Belmas
Designed by Katrina Newby
Illustrations by Deborah Peyton

Printed in China

Acknowledgments

This book was a challenge. Although the ideas flooded in and the testing of techniques and designs progressed smoothly, my personal life kept interfering with the deadlines. The obligations of motherhood, travel, and, oh yes, my full time job at *Designs in Machine Embroidery* magazine, kept getting me sidetracked. You wouldn't be holding this book in your hands if it weren't for the patience and perseverance of my colleagues at Krause Publications, Candy Wiza, Acquisitions Editor and Andy Belmas, Associate Editor. I am very grateful for their professionalism, wisdom, and guidance. Thank you, Candy and Andy.

And there are others to whom I owe gratitude. First, Nancy Zieman. Nancy has been a guiding light in my life, both professionally and personally for many years. I was thrilled to share the contents of this book on *Sewing with Nancy*—during her 25th season, no less! It is a privilege to be a guest on SWN, but to be a part of its 25-year milestone is truly an honor. Thank you, Nancy.

Of course I'd like to thank my children. Janelle and Ted, I continue to be impressed by your accomplishments. The challenges that you take on and the hurdles you have both overcome have made you into a fine young woman and man. It has been a blast parenting you and watching you grow. There has never been a dull moment, and I couldn't be more proud of you than I am today.

Marie Zinno, my younger, blond twin (not really twins but definitely sisters) has been with me through thick and thin. She has listened to it all, laughed and cried, encouraged and scolded, and cheered me on. I wouldn't be here without her faith in me and I probably wouldn't want to be.

Lastly, I am grateful to a new person in my life, Pete, for putting the word joy back into my world.

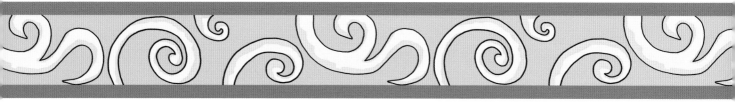

Contents

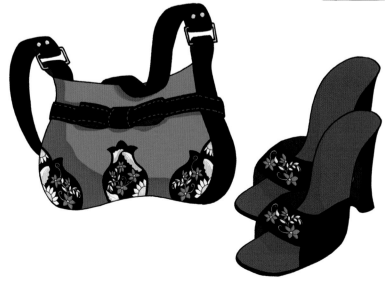

Introduction

Handbags, belts, and shoes! Can a girl ever have enough accessories? Now you don't have to answer that question—just get stitching—you'll love what's in store for you.

Originally, I planned to have all the projects in this book coordinate with the projects in my previous book, *Contemporary Machine-Embroidered Fashions* (Krause, 2006). But you know what happens when you start a new project, it takes on a life of its own. I realized that I could give you a more diverse embroidery experience by going off in a new direction. So off I went.

The new direction opened up a flood of new ideas, and I had a blast sketching, experimenting, tweaking, and perfecting. A whole new concept was born—Functional Embroidery. Functional Embroidery is a lot like you—it not only looks good, but it works, too! This book features two new techniques that really simplify purse-making and guarantee professional results. What a powerful combination that is!

The first technique in Functional Embroidery is embroidered appliqué designs that actually create the shape of the bag. You'll stitch two designs on a rectangle of fabric, one for the bag front and one for the back. Then you'll sew the front and back to a gusset using the embroidery as the seam line. It may sound complicated, but all you really need to know how to do is cut a rectangle and sew on a line.

The second technique is purse handle "anchor" designs. These decorative details secure the handle to the bag. I love the little splash of embroidery this technique adds to each bag. The anchor designs are easy to complete—just stitch, trim the appliqué, fold the wings, and stitch again.

And what is a beautiful bag without matching shoes and belts? We have some lovely, delicate designs perfect for tiny spaces on shoes. And you'll learn how to embellish a belt buckle or just stitch a belt band.

Follow along as I illustrate how simple it is to use your embroidery machine to make beautiful, professional accessories.

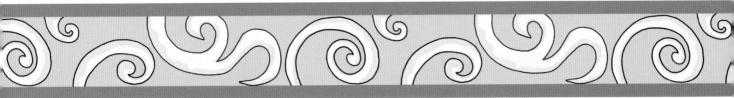

Chapter 1 # What You Need to Know

The Elements

Size Does Matter

What's the difference between a "great bag" and a "just ok" bag? It can be as little as two inches! As I researched and designed the bags in this book, I learned it's all about size. It's the size of the bag and length of the handles that make or break a bag. I was amazed at what a difference one or two inches can make on both appeal and function, and that's just on the bag itself. The make or break mark for the embroidery designs can be as narrow as half an inch.

When designing your bag, measure your current favorite satchel and use it as a guideline for your next creation. The bags (and measurements) in this book work for me—they fit all the stuff I have to carry, they slide under my arm, and they look great! To make them work for you, use measurements from your current favorite bag and adapt them to my instructions. After all, a custom bag should fit you perfectly and make you look fabulous.

Of course, it's not just about size—it's about starting with the right materials. Don't chintz on the elements; buy the best fabrics, stabilizers and findings you can afford. Remember, a good bag is a constant companion and it will get lots of wear and tear. Starting with "good stuff" will just add to the life of the bag.

Fabrics
Faux Suede

Today's faux suede and faux leather are extraordinary. They look and feel like the real thing but cost half the money. Most are easy to care for and machine washable. I love the texture of these faux fabrics, and the wide variety of colors and finishes. These fabrics make my bags look professional. You'll never have to settle for the offerings of department stores again, now you can be the designer—and embroider it yourself!

Canvas

Canvas is a strong, durable natural fiber material. I love the natty surface of canvas and think it adds a casual flair to most bags. I also like how it washes and ages—it's like a favorite pair of blue jeans with fibers that soften with time. And as a girl who grew up on the Jersey shore, it always reminds me of the beach, my favorite place on the planet.

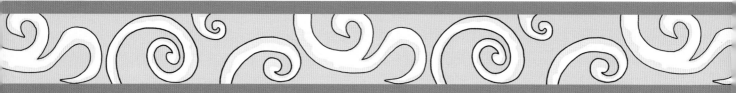

Lining

I line all my bags—mainly to hide unsightly seam allowances and bobbin threads. I use cotton or linen fabrics in a medium color for lining my bags. I've taken my cue from the auto industry here—if you look at the carpeting in most of today's automobiles, you'll notice it's usually not dark or light, but more of a medium tone. This helps camouflage dirt since it's the same tone as most dirt. Even though I don't step into my bags—they sure do get a lot of "traffic!" So I don't want a light colored lining—as the bag would appear dingy very quickly. And I don't want a dark colored lining, because then I wouldn't be able to find anything in it!

Interfacing

Some faux suede fabrics are lightweight and can use a little stiffening to help shape the bag. I cut Pellon ShirTailor to the finished size of the bag, eliminating any interfacing in the seam allowances. Follow the manufacturer's directions for fusing the ShirTailor to the wrong side of the faux suede.

Stabilizers

A wide variety of stabilizers are available at your local sewing machine dealer or fabric store and on the internet. Always keep a supply of cut-away, tear-away, and water-soluble stabilizers in your sewing room. For many of the projects in this book, I have used Stitch N Shape fusible stabilizer. Since the combination of embroidery designs and fabrics vary with every project, so will the stabilizer requirements. It's best to have a selection of different weights on hand.

Templates—Don't Stitch Without 'Em!

A template is a printed image of an embroidery design in actual size with the center of the design clearly marked. The more I embroider, the more I value templates. I am truly uncomfortable when I have to embroider "blindly"—without templates! I've done it on occasion, but it wasn't fun. So where do you get templates? Today, you get them from your embroidery software. They are so easy to make—any embroidery software program will let you select File > Print when you have a design on the screen. Just insert tracing paper or a transparency into your printer and voila—you have a template.

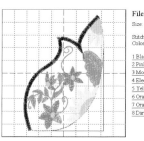

Filename: MEA19.pes
Size: 64 x 91 mm
2.52 x 3.58 in
Stitches: 5966
Colors: 8

1 Black
2 Pink
3 Moss Green
4 Electric Blue
5 Yellow
6 Orange
7 Orange
8 Dark Brown

There are two areas of focus when working with embroidery designs. When I designed the handbags, I focused on the outer edges of an embroidery design. These edges create the shape of the bag, so I needed to know exactly where the outside edges would land.

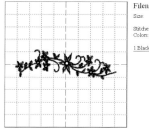

Filename: MEA21.pes
Size: 82 x 23 mm
3.23 x 0.91 in
Stitches: 2704
Colors: 1

1 Black

When I designed the embroidery layout for the Continuous Vine belt, I was concerned with where one design ended and where the next one began. The embroidery on the belt appears to be a continuous line. In reality, it is not a continuous line, it's multiple hoopings with precise placement—perfected with the use of templates. Centering horizontal designs on a belt is also simplified by the printed image of the design.

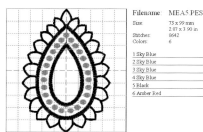

Filename: MEA5.PES
Size: 73 x 99 mm
2.87 x 3.90 in
Stitches: 8642
Colors: 6

1 Sky Blue
2 Sky Blue
3 Sky Blue
4 Sky Blue
5 Black
6 Amber Red

The other area of focus is the center of the design. If a design must land in the center of a flap, first I find the center of the flap, then I position the center of the template on that mark.

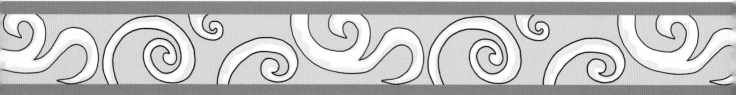

Other Helpful Tools

Over the many years that I've immersed myself in this hobby, I've often been frustrated at the lack of tools available for machine embroiderers. Machine embroidery is highly technical and great advances have been made in machine features, software and media, but little attention is paid to the actual process of getting the fabric in the hoop and the design where you want it to land! I've created a few products that simplify the embroidery process. I think you'll find them helpful, too.

Target Stickers

Target stickers are small, pressure sensitive adhesive stickers that eliminate the need to mark the fabric. Printed with cross hairs and an arrow, these target stickers can be used over and over again. Slide the target under a taped template, aligning the cross hairs of the sticker with the template's cross hairs. Once the sticker is secure, remove the template and hoop the fabric. Now you don't have to worry about shifting templates during the hooping process or erasing any marks left by "removable" markers.

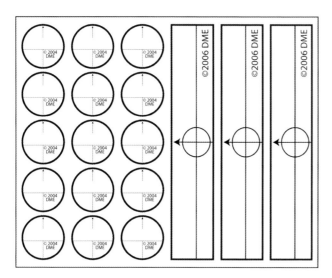

Angle Finder

If you hoop the fabric wrong, you can still stitch it straight! The Angle Finder will tell you exactly how much rotation is required to stitch the embroidery design as planned. With the combination of templates, target stickers, and the Angle Finder, every design will stitch perfectly straight. Just follow these easy instructions for hooping wrong and stitching right! The Angle Finder works with any machine that features one degree or five degree rotation.

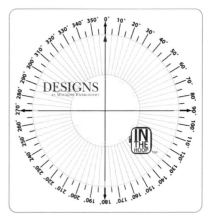

1. Position a template and target sticker on the fabric in the desired location. Hoop the fabric, don't worry about hooping perfectly square. Center the Angle Finder on the target sticker with the zero-degree mark degree facing towards the upper edge of the hoop.

2. Keep the Angle Finder's black cross hairs square to the hoop's outer edges. Rotate the dial on the Angle Finder so that the red cross hairs are aligned with the target sticker.

3. Note the rotation degree that the red arrow designates. Make sure both arrows (target sticker and red cross hairs) are facing in the same direction.

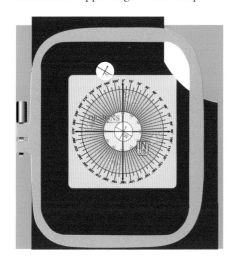

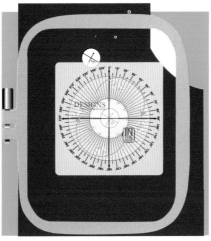

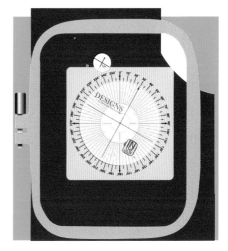

4. Rotate the design on the screen using the rotation keys until you reach the number as illustrated on the Angle Finder.

5. Embroider the design.

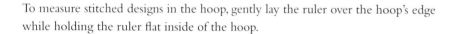

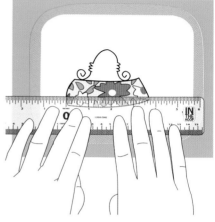

Centering Rulers

Use a centering ruler to measure the size of stitched designs, distances between existing designs, and to mark vertical and horizontal positioning lines. The rulers work on both flat surfaces and in the hoop. Their flexibility allows you to accurately measure inside the restricted area of a hoop. Their translucency enables you to see existing markings, target stickers, embroidery designs, or sewn seams clearly.

To measure stitched designs in the hoop, gently lay the ruler over the hoop's edge while holding the ruler flat inside of the hoop.

To repeat a pattern:

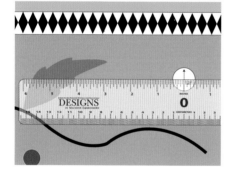

1. Measure the size of the stitched design and divide by two. Measure the distance between the two designs. Add half the design size measurement plus the distance between the designs to find the center point for the third design. Place that measurement on the outer edge of the second design.

2. Place a target sticker on the zero mark. Center the needle over the target sticker cross hairs, remove the sticker, and embroider the design.

To stitch continuous hoop designs:

1. Even if you don't have a continuous hoop, you can still create continuous hoop designs with a centering ruler. Stitch the first design. Measure the design by placing one outer edge of the design on the zero.

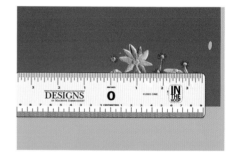

2. Note the size (3½") and divide that number by two (1¾"). Place a target sticker on the 1¾" mark on the opposite side of the zero. Move the fabric in the hoop so that the target sticker is located under the needle. Embroider the design and repeat the process.

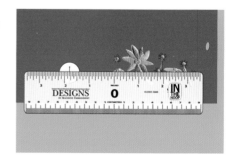

Magna-Hoop

I try to avoid using adhesive stabilizers or temporary spray adhesive on fashion embroidery. It's a personal decision—I just don't like the sticky residue on my garments, handbags, belts, or hoops, so I was thrilled to develop a new product: Magna-Hoop. It hoops the unhoopable—things that are oddly shaped or too small to fit in a hoop, and it's perfect for the challenge of specialty fabrics like velvet, silk, leather, faux leather, etc. Hoop burn is virtually eliminated with Magna-Hoop. It's so easy to use, you'll be amazed at its simplicity and effectiveness.

1. Just hoop stabilizer (tear-away, wash-away, or cut-away) as you normally would.

2. Insert the Magna-Hoop metal frame into the hoop.

3. Position the item on the hoop.

4. Place the appropriate acrylic frame on top (Magna-Hoop comes with five different acrylic frames). Snap the magnets into the slots and you're ready to stitch.

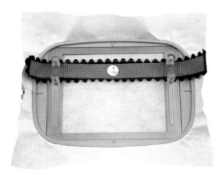

Magna-Hoop comes with five acrylic frames, each with a different opening to accommodate a variety of items and designs.

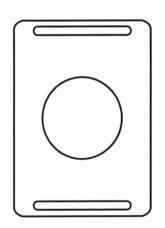

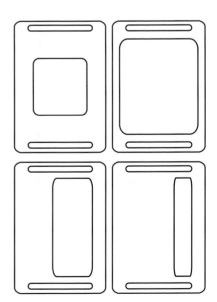

Machines

There are many different embroidery machines available today with prices ranging from $300 to over $8000. Why such a disparity in price? The answer is in the features. An embroidery machine can be a stand-alone unit or a combination of sewing and embroidery. It can have a computer built inside or it can be powered by a desktop or laptop computer. A home embroidery machine will have one needle and can usually accommodate a number of hoop sizes.

So where does one start when purchasing an embroidery machine? Hopefully, right in your hometown. Embroidery machines can be highly technical; a helpful, knowledgeable sewing machine dealer who is located close to you is worth her weight in gold. Don't necessarily shop by brand, shop by dealer. Visit several local dealers and select the one who offers education, has on-site repairs and is someone you enjoy visiting. Then test drive! Decide what features are important to you and sit down at several models in your price range. Take the machine through some common tasks, such as selecting an embroidery design and making a few on-screen edits. If you feel comfortable with the screen, the layout, the keys, etc., this could be the machine for you.

There are a few luxurious features that one may enjoy but are not absolutely necessary. They are automatic threading systems, automatic thread trimmers, low bobbin indicators, and the ability to read multiple formats.

Of course, the number one feature is the stitch quality. Your embroidery machine should present you with beautiful embroidery, so look for it when shopping for a new machine. Below are a few machine features I can't live without.

Media: I love an embroidery machine that accepts a USB memory stick because it goes right from my computer to the machine. And I'm looking forward to a universal wireless transfer in the future.

Hoop movement: Since I do most of my design editing at my computer, the most important feature for me at the machine is the ability to position the needle over any spot in the hoop. I say "position the needle" even though the needle does not move, the hoop moves. And I want to see the needle positioned directly over a target sticker or template before I take a stitch.

On-screen editing: A highly-visible LCD screen makes selecting and editing designs a breeze. I like seeing the design on screen in full color.

Perimeter tracing: This feature travels around the outer-most edges of a design without taking a stitch. It's helpful when checking accuracy in placement.

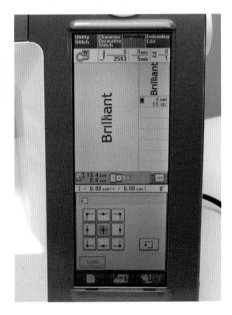

Hoop size: A maximum 5" x 7" sewing field is the smallest field that I would consider when purchasing an embroidery machine. The larger sewing fields (7" x 10" and larger) are helpful but not mandatory, so skimp here if your budget is tight.

Mirror image: This cuts down on computer design time and transfer time.

One-degree rotation: I couldn't live without the ability to rotate in tiny increments.

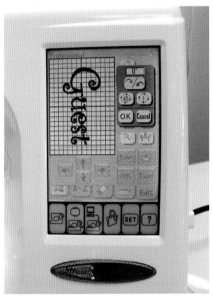

Findings

Purse handles: I like handles that feature rings on the end. Then, I make fabric or webbing loops to attach the handle to the bag. No messy hardware, just a simple loop and ring.

Belt buckles: Solid metal belt buckles with an open, oval, or round shape are the perfect landing spot for embroidery. Embroidered inlays are a simple way to add texture and color to an outfit.

Magnetic snap closures: Magnetic snap closures are the professional way to close a bag and they are, uh, pardon the pun, a snap to apply. Magnetic snaps are made of four pieces, the male and female sides plus two metal braces that reinforce the snap.

To apply a magnetic snap closure:

1. *Mark the position of the snap on both sides of the bag or the flap and bag.*

3. *Place the metal brace over the mark and mark inside both slots.*

5. *Slide the metal brace over the prongs on the wrong side of the fabric.*

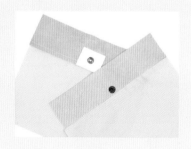

2. *Reinforce the area with strong interfacing or Stitch N Shape fusible stabilizer.*

4. *Make a slit on each mark. Insert the snap, prongs first, into the slits.*

6. *Fold the prongs over the metal brace. Repeat for the piece opposite of the snap.*

Notions

A well-equipped sewing room or embroidery studio makes sewing and stitching a delight. The notions below are always within arm's reach in my work area. And yes, that means I probably own more than one of each!

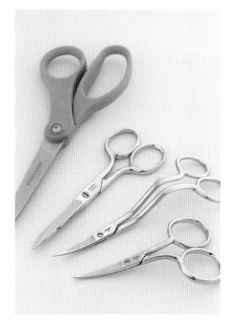

* needles
* seam ripper
* appliqué scissors
* curved-tip embroidery scissors
* rotary cutter
* pins
* paper clips (for working with faux leather and suede)
* quilter's ruler with a 45-degree angle
* cutting mat
* Chalk-O-Liner
* eyelet cutter
* awl
* Fasturn

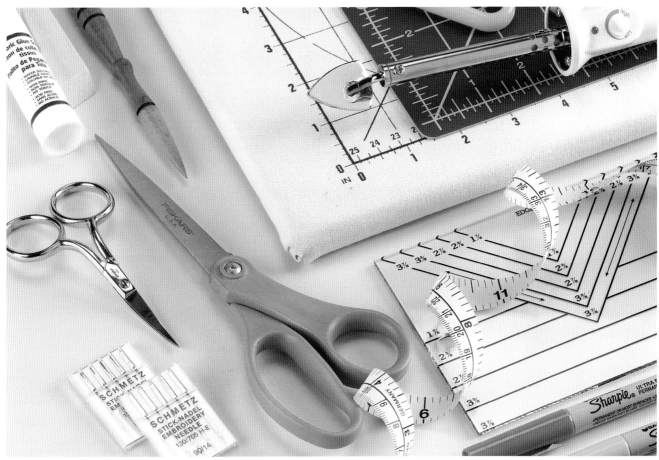

Embroidery Designs

There are thousands of embroidery designs available to you. You can find them in your embroidery machine, at your local dealership and on the Internet. Embroidery designs are available on CD (like the designs included in this book), floppy disk, flash stick, memory card, wireless connectivity, and direct connection with a computer. They come in many popular formats including ART, DST, EXP, HUS, JEF, PCS, PES, SEW, SHV, and XXX, among others. Read your embroidery machine manual to determine the format and media that your machine requires.

The embroidery designs in this book were drawn specifically for accessories—bags, belts, and shoes. Although you may find other uses for them, they have been designed to fit in specific areas. Most of the designs are what I call "functional embroidery." Not only are the embroidery designs beautiful adornments, but they work as construction elements, too!

The corner appliqué designs create the final shape of the bag—no sewing pattern required.

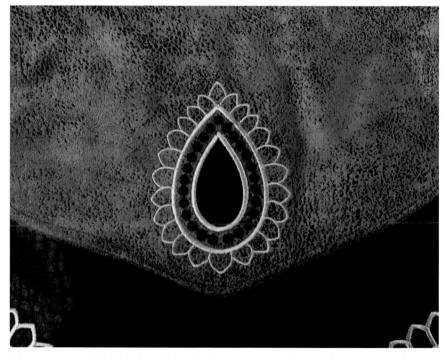

The center medallion designs fit perfectly on a flap and conceal a magnetic closure underneath.

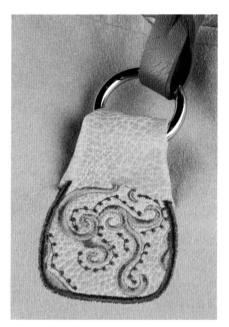

The tiny shoe embellishment designs add a soft touch to any shoe. The horizontal border designs fit snugly into a 1½" belt. And finally, the belt buckle design is that little extra that some ensembles need. The designs are in six formats and all fit in a standard 4" x 4" hoop so any machine can create these projects. A larger hoop will speed things up but is not a necessity.

The tab designs hold the shoulder strap in place.

Preparing the Designs

You will need an embroidery editing software program (also known as customizing software) with the following features:

* Copy and paste
* Sizing with stitch recalculation
* 360-degree rotation
* Mirror image
* Color sort
* View by color
* Lasso tool
* Sew simulator
* Print

Some familiar brands of customizing software are Buzz Tools, Buzz Edit, Stitch Editor (Husqvarna Viking), Bernina Editor, PE-Design (Brother), Generations, Origins, Explorations (OESD), Designer's Gallery Studio (Baby Lock), Pfaff Creative Stitch Editor, Digitizer 10000 (Janome), Professional Sew Ware (Singer), Amazing Designs Edit N Stitch.

Opening a Design

1. Insert the enclosed CD into your CD-ROM drive.

2. Open your embroidery software. When the embroidery software is open, select File > Open.

3. Select the CD-ROM drive from the menu that appears.

4. Select the folder with the format that is compatible with your embroidery machine. If you don't know what file format to use with your embroidery machine, check the machine manual or call the store that sold you the machine and ask.

5. Select design MEA19. Notice that the design name will be followed by a dot and the abbreviation of your format. Your embroidery software recognizes the dot and the abbreviation as an embroidery file.

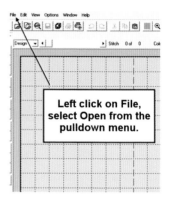

Left click on File, select Open from the pulldown menu.

On-Screen Information

* The size of the design is 65 mm x 91 mm. This is helpful when determining if the design will fit in the allotted space.
* The position of the design in the sewing field or hoop is also listed. The default setting is in the center, 0 mm x 0 mm on the XY axis. If you move the design, the position of the design center will also change.
* Also, the stitch count is visible (5900) along with the number of color changes (eight).
* To select the design, move the cursor onto the design and left click. Notice the design has a "box" around it with a "handle" on each corner.

Software Tools

Copy and Paste

The copy and paste function enables you to duplicate and merge separate embroidery designs into one file. Click on the design to select it, go to File > Copy (or CTRL C) and File > Paste (or CTRL V).

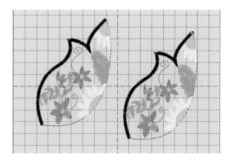

Sizing

The sizing function enables you to adjust the size of an embroidery design while adding and subtracting stitches automatically. Keep in mind that the detail in an embroidery design is determined by its original size. A butterfly originally digitized at 2½" will look very simplistic when enlarged to 4½". The opposite is also true; a highly detailed butterfly digitized at 4½" will be too busy at 2½".

While holding the shift key, click on the embroidery design and drag one corner handle to make the design larger or smaller. Holding the shift key will maintain the design proportions.

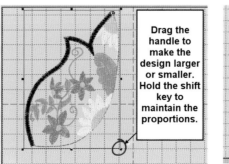

Drag the handle to make the design larger or smaller. Hold the shift key to maintain the proportions.

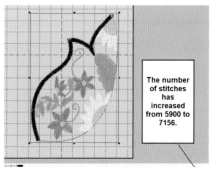

The number of stitches has increased from 5900 to 7156.

Rotation

The rotation tool spins the design. To use it, click on the rotation tool icon. Then click on the embroidery design to select and move one corner of the design in the desired direction.

Click on the rotation tool, click on the embroidery design to select it, and move one corner of the design to rotate it in the desired position.

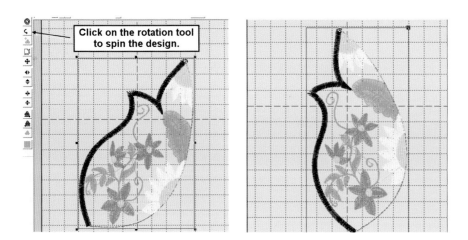

Click on the rotation tool to spin the design.

Mirror Image

The mirror image tool duplicates the embroidery design in mirror image horizontally or vertically.

Click on the embroidery design to select it and click on the mirror image tool (vertical or horizontal option).

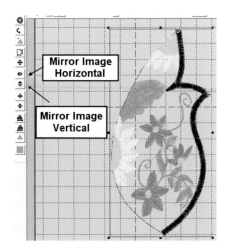

Mirror Image Horizontal

Mirror Image Vertical

Color Sort

The color sort tool merges all like colors into one color segment. It is especially helpful when repeating the same design in one hoop.

To use the color sort tool, copy and paste the designs onto the screen in the desired positions. Click on color sort.

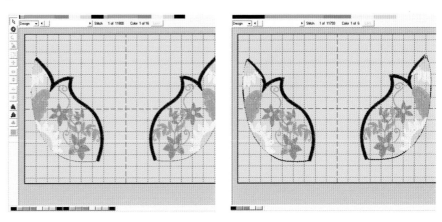

This option should be used with caution as the sequencing of the color segments can be affected. Use the sew simulator to check for accuracy if your software program has that feature. As a rule of thumb, designs that contain the same colors and that overlap each other may cause trouble when the color sort feature is used. If the designs do not overlap, color sort will eliminate unnecessary thread changes. Whenever you do use color sort, make sure you use the Save As command to change the file name without overriding the original design.

View by Color

View by color lets you travel through the design—color segment by color segment—and lets you select, remove, or duplicate a segment.

Click on the design to select it and click on the view by color tool. Click on the tool to travel through the design.

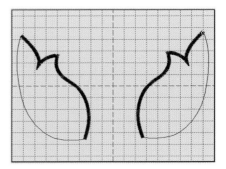

Organizing and Storing Designs

Organizing your embroidery designs in your computer helps you access your designs quickly. Since many embroidery designs are labeled by number, it's difficult to remember the correct title of each individual design, making design location a tedious process. I have a few suggestions to help you get organized.

For this collection, it would be best to store the CD in the sleeve provided in the back of this book. For all other collections, purchase a three-ring binder, CD and floppy-disk storage sleeves, and a three-hole punch from any office supply store. Upon opening a disk collection, punch holes in the artwork (and the packaging and thread list if applicable). Insert the artwork in the binder and the CD or floppy into the storage sleeve. As time passes, you'll love the convenience of going to the binder and locating the exact collection by looking at the printed pages.

Storing Designs on a Hard Drive

Let me show you how I organized my hard drive for creating this book. To access the hard drive (which happens to be the C drive on my computer), go to Start > My Computer. Then double click on the icon for the C drive.

Next, create a new folder titled Embroidery Designs. To create a new folder, right click on the screen, and select New > Folder. Type in Embroidery Designs.

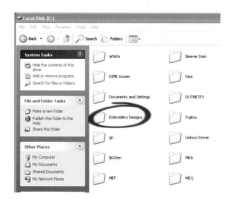

On my computer, I've created a number of categories in the Embroidery Designs folder. I've listed some collections by name, such as the Designs Interactive CD 1, 2, and 3. That's logical for me because they are collections that I've personally designed so it's easy to remember exactly what embroidery files are in each collection. Other files are labeled Flowers, Trees, Animals, Geometrics, and so on. Each folder has subcategories when opened. For instance, in Animals, you'll find Cats, Dogs, Fish, Wildlife, etc. The more definitive you are, the easier it is to locate files.

Let's take a look in the Machine-Embroidered Accessories folder on my computer.

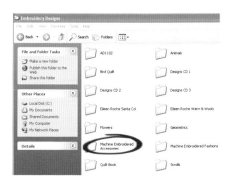

First, double click on the folder to open it. Each category, or chapter, in Machine-Embroidered Accessories is listed by name.

I've stored all of the original designs and manipulated designs that are required for that category. In doing this, some designs are in multiple locations. Let's look in the Bags and Belts folder. Every design featured in that category is in that folder.

When I start a new project, I create a new folder with the project name. Then I open my embroidery software and access the designs from their original source, which could be another file from the main Embroidery Design folder, or from a CD or floppy disk. As I manipulate the designs, I save them in the new folder.

This system helps me keep track of my work as it develops. And I hope you find it helpful, too!

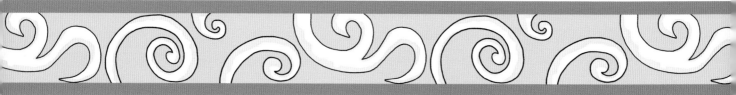

Chapter 2 Bags and Belts

Secrets to Success

✻ Use the best fabrics you can find. Real suede and leather are quite luxurious but many faux materials feel and look as good as the real thing.

✻ Select neutral-colored linings to avoid dingy interiors.

✻ Hunt for interesting findings: d-rings, handles, and other findings can really add spunk and originality to a bag.

✻ Look at the overall design of the bag before adding bling—the idea is to enhance, not overwhelm, the small stature of belts, buckles, and embroidery designs.

✻ Speaking of bling—look beyond the crystals. Metal nailheads are available in a slew of colors and shapes. They may not sparkle as much as crystal but they add interest to borders, flower centers, and more. Experiment with a variety of shapes and colors.

✻ Work with the basic form of a buckle (oval, circular, square, or rectangular) to create your original design. To avoid glaring mishaps, keep the embroidery asymmetrical. Use bling or small decorative cording to fill in any gaps between the fabric and metal border.

Sand and Sea Bag

This nifty embroidery design, MEA3, is what I call Functional Embroidery. It's not only pretty, it works, too! The appliqué design actually secures the handle to the bag. How cool is that?

I selected the gentle colors of one my favorite beaches in Sanibel, Florida to create the Sand and Sea bag. The soft aqua faux suede reminds me of the gentle waves of the Gulf of Mexico while the supple, faux-leather handle anchor designs bring thoughts of the sand. The combination of great color, supple textures, and a great technique makes this bag a sure hit. Try it yourself; you'll be amazed how easy this new technique is. And you'll love the professional results—your bag will look like you bought it at a high-end department store.

Materials

* ⅓ yd. faux suede
* ¼ yd. faux leather
* ⅓ yd. lining fabric
* ⅔ yd. Pellon ShirTailor interfacing
* Cut-away stabilizer
* Magnetic snap closure
* Protective pressing sheet
* Scraps of Stitch N Shape Double fusible stabilizer
* Two 23" faux leather or leather purse handles with rings
* MEA3 embroidery design and two MEA3 templates

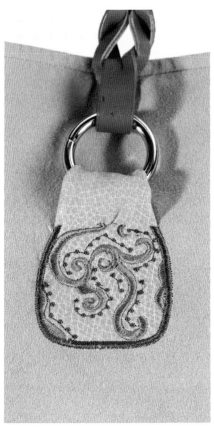

Cut

* From the faux suede, cut two 14½" x 12" pieces for the bag's front and back
* From the faux leather, cut four 4" squares (appliqué) and two 14½" x 3½" (facing)
* From the lining, cut two 14½" x 9½" pieces
* From the Pellon ShirTailor interfacing, cut two 13½" x 11" pieces

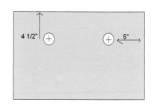

Prepare

1. Center and fuse the Pellon ShirTailor interfacing pieces to the wrong side of the two 14½" x 12" pieces of faux suede.

2. Lay the two templates on the 14½" x 12" faux suede. The center of each template is 4½" from the top and 5" from the outside edge. Slide target stickers under the templates and remove the templates.

Embroider

1. Hoop the cut-away stabilizer. Insert the Magna-Hoop metal frame in the hoop. Place the faux suede on the hoop along with the Magna-Hoop large rectangular acrylic frame. Snap the magnets into place.

2. Attach the hoop to the machine. Stitch the first color of the design, the placement guide. Place a 4" square of faux leather over the design area. Position the square so that the bottom edge of the square sits just below the bottom edge of the outline.

Stitch the second color, the tackdown. Remove the hoop from the machine, but don't remove the fabric from the hoop.

3. Place the straight edge of a ruler at the top of the appliqué. Draw a line from the stitches to the outside edge. Slit the appliqué fabric on the drawn lines, stopping at the stitching line to create the "wings."

4. Carefully trim away the excess faux leather from the appliqué stopping at the drawn lines.

5. Fold the wings as shown below.

6. Slide the folded wings through the ring of the handle.

7. Insert the folded wings into the appliqué pocket.

8. Place the hoop back on the machine and embroider the design.

Repeat for the three remaining target stickers.

An Alternate Method For Appliqué

1. To save time, consider cutting all four appliqué sections before hooping the bag. No need to measure or draw, just use the embroidery design to stitch the perfect outline of the appliqué. Let me show you how easy it is to do.

2. In the editing feature of your embroidery machine, load four repeats of design MEA3 into one hoop, placing the designs a least ¾" apart. Hoop tear-away stabilizer. Stitch only the first color, the placement guide, of the first design on the hooped stabilizer. Advance through the colors until you reach the first color of the second design. Stitch the first color and repeat this process for the remaining designs.

3. Go back to the first color of the first design. Place a 4" square of faux leather on the appliqué outline, placing the bottom edge of the square just below the bottom of the appliqué. Stitch color #1 again.

4. Advance to the first color of the second design, place a 4" square of faux leather on the appliqué. Make sure no portion of the first square is lying in the appliqué area of design #2. Stitch the first color of the second design.

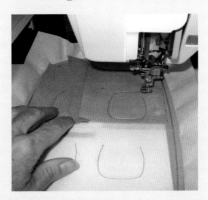

5. Repeat for the remaining appliqués.

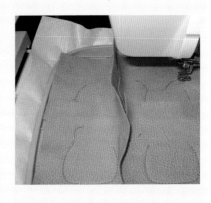

6. Remove the hoop from the machine and the stabilizer from the hoop. Carefully remove the tear-away stabilizer without distorting the appliqué pieces.

7. Hoop one of the bag sections and center the first target sticker under the needle. Stitch the first color of the appliqué design. Dab the interior of the appliqué area with a glue stick. Finger press the cut appliqué section on the bag, aligning the edges of the cut appliqué with the stitched outline. Stitch color #2, the tackdown, and complete the design as outlined above. Repeat for the remaining designs.

Assemble

1. Sew the bag sections together at the sides and bottom.

2. Press open all seam allowances. Fold the corner, matching the side seam to the bottom seam. Stitch through all layers, creating a "square" bottom.

3. Sew the lining to the facing, right sides together.

4. Mark the position of the magnetic snap, 2½" down from the center of the top of the facing. Fuse a scrap of Stitch N Shape Double fusible stabilizer to this area. Apply one half of the magnetic snap.

5. Sew the lining sections together at the sides and bottom, leaving a 4" opening in the bottom.

6. Press the seam allowances open. Fold the corner, matching the side seam to the bottom seam. Stitch through all layers, creating a "square" bottom as in Step 2.

7. Turn the bag wrong side out. Turn the lining right side out. Insert the lining into the bag, matching the side seams. Pin the upper edge keeping the handles out of the way. Sew with ½" seam allowance. Turn the bag right side out through the opening in the bottom of the lining.

8. Press the seam.

9. Using a topstitch needle, sew around the upper edge of the bag, ½" from the edge.

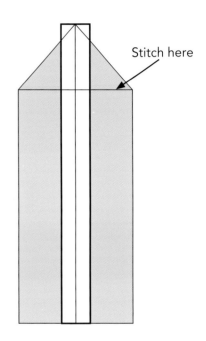

Stitch here

Try Wearing With...

Nautical stripe t-shirt with a boat neck, white gauze pants, light athletic shoes

Alternate Color Idea

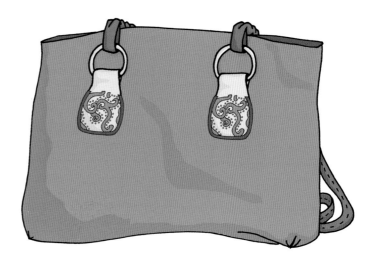

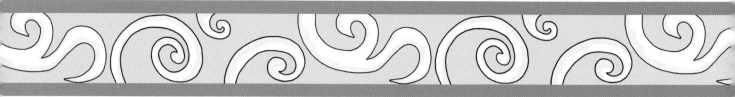

Sand and Sea Belt

Belts add such a nice finishing touch to jeans, dresses, and more. The combination of a matching bag and belt shows you've invested quite some thought into your ensemble. And when you make both the bag and the belt, you can control everything—the colors, the fabrics, the hardware, and the fit. Consider making a variety of belts that coordinate with the bag—they'll give the bag more legs and you'll have the option of wearing a dark or light belt. On my short stature, I often opt for a monochromatic look. I can still wear a decorative belt; I just make sure the base fabric is in the same color value as the outfit, avoiding that "cut in half" look.

Materials

* Faux leather: 5" x waist measurement plus 8"
* Polymesh stabilizer
* 1½" belt backing or belt webbing (waist measurement plus 6")
* One belt buckle
* Awl or eyelet cutter
* MEA23 embroidery design and three MEA23 templates
* Magna-Hoop with medium acrylic rectangle frame
* Fasturn

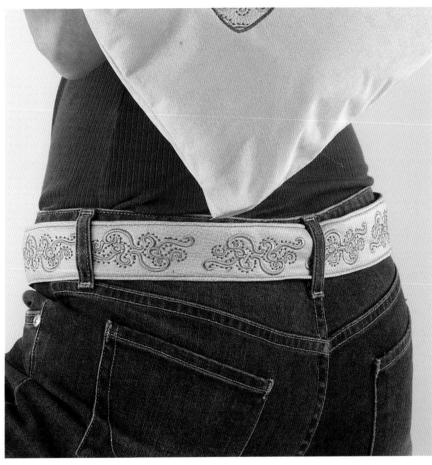

Prepare

1. Measure your waist or hip and add 8" to the amount. Cut the faux leather that measurement.

2. Place a piece of tape 4½" from one end and 2" from the opposite end. Write "Buckle" on the tape that is 2" from the end.

Leave 2" blank at one end.

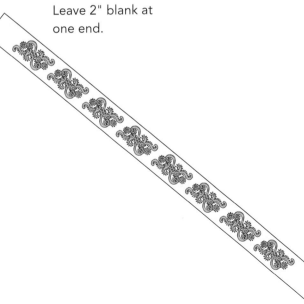

Leave 4½" blank at the other end.

35

Embroider

1. Center the MEA23 templates on the width of the faux leather strip starting at the "Buckle" tape mark. Place the top edge of the embroidery design on the tape. Evenly space the remaining templates about ¼" apart. Slide a target sticker under each template and remove the templates.

2. Hoop polymesh stabilizer in the largest hoop available. Insert the Magna-Hoop metal frame. Position the first template on the hoop. Place the medium acrylic frame over the fabric, centering a template in the opening. Snap the magnets in place.

3. Attach the hoop to the machine and position the needle over the first target sticker. Embroider the designs.

4. Remove the faux leather from the hoop and lay it right side up on a flat surface.

5. Place the edge of a quilter's ruler on the outside edge of the embroidery, extending the length of the ruler into the next area to be embroidered. Place the templates along the edge of the ruler, evenly spacing them as in the first group of embroidered designs. This will help you place and stitch the embroidery in a straight line. Slide target stickers under the templates and remove the templates.

6. Hoop polymesh stabilizer and the faux leather, centering the target stickers. Continue embroidering the designs as in Steps 2 and 3. Repeat until the belt is completely embroidered, reaching as close as possible to the tape.

7. Remove the tape, but note which end is the buckle end.

Assemble

1. Trim all excess stabilizer and thread tails.

2. Use a quilter's ruler to trim the strip to a 4" width, centering the embroidery in the strip. Fold the strip in half lengthwise, right sides together, and sew the long edge with a ½" seam allowance.

3. Carefully center the seam allowance in the strip and press the seam allowance open using a protective pressing sheet.

4. Turn the tube, right side out, using a Fasturn.

5. Slide the belt backing or webbing into the tube.

6. Fold in the raw edges on each end and pin.

7. Topstitch the ends shut.

8. Slide the buckle end of the belt onto the buckle ring.

9. Topstitch through all layers of the belt to secure the buckle to the belt.

10. Try on the belt and mark the hole(s) for the point of the buckle.

11. Use an awl or eyelet cutter to cut the hole.

Try Wearing With...

Khakis, blazer, sensible walking shoes

Denim dress with a belted waist, strappy sandals

Alternate Color Idea

Swirly Slouch Bag

A few years ago, lime green seemed to explode into our world of design. Paired with black, it became the new beige. Today, it's softened into an apple green. Apple green seems a bit more sophisticated than the earlier version of screaming lime, and it's compatible with many colors. A fresh twist—shown here in the Swirly Slouch bag—is brown, apple green, and beige.

The embroidery embellishes only the straps, taking a step away from traditional embroidered bags. On a business trip to San Diego in June, 2006, I spotted a stylish woman in the lobby of a swank hotel. Slung over her shoulder was a leather satchel that had the most interesting strap. Naturally, I followed her across the floor to get a closer glimpse at her bag. I didn't stop her, but I did stop long enough to sketch the satchel on a yes, you guessed it, a napkin! Months later, that sketch gave life to the Swirly Slouch bag. Enjoy!

Materials

* ⅓ yd. dark brown canvas
* ½ yd. faux suede
* ⅓ yd. lining fabric
* Polymesh stabilizer
* Stitch N Shape Double fusible stabilizer
* Protective pressing sheet
* Tracing paper or transparency templates of MEA10, MEA11 and MEA12

Cut

❋ From the brown canvas, cut one 4" x 36" strip for the shoulder strap; one 4" x 17" strip for the tab closure; two 4" squares for the decorative patches

❋ From the faux suede, cut two 16" x 17" pieces for the body using the pattern on page 126 for top curve, two 16" x 5" for the facing using the pattern piece on page 126 for top curve

❋ From the lining, cut two 16" x 13" pieces

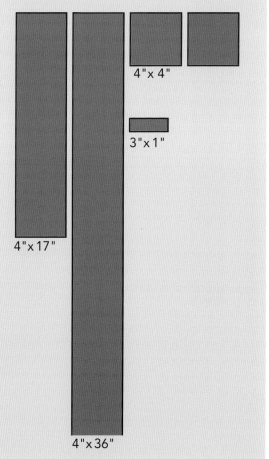

4" x 4"

3" x 1"

4" x 17"

4" x 36"

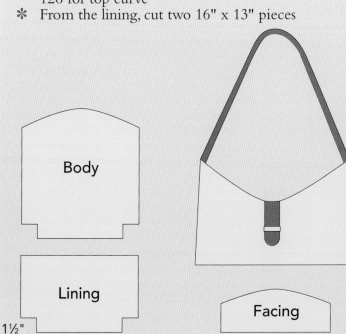

Body

Lining

1½"

Facing

Embroider

1. Place the 4" x 36" strip of brown canvas, right side down, on a pressing surface.

2. Cut a strip of Stitch N Shape fusible stabilizer 1½" x 36". Place the stabilizer strip, glue side down, on the 4" x 36" strip of brown canvas as shown below.

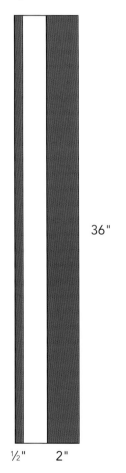

36"

½"   2"

3. Fuse the stabilizer to the fabric. Flip the fabric over and press from the right side. This will make an indentation of the stabilizer, making it easy to locate the edges of the stabilizer strip.

4. Place the templates on the strip, evenly spacing the designs within the edges of the stabilizer. Slide a target sticker under each template. Remove the templates, one at a time, and write the design number on the target sticker. Repeat until the entire strip is full, leaving 3" blank spaces at each end. The sample has twelve designs.

5. Hoop the fused fabric and polymesh stabilizer in the largest (longest!) hoop available.

6. Attach the hoop to the machine and center the needle over the cross hairs of the first target sticker. If your machine has the trace feature, use it now to ensure the design is centered within the stabilizer area of the strip. Embroider the first design. Position the needle over the next cross hairs, remove the target sticker, and complete the design. Repeat for each design.

7. Rehoop as necessary, repeating the steps above until all twelve designs are stitched.

8. Trim the excess polymesh stabilizer.

9. Place the embroidered strip, right side down, on a pressing surface. Fold the ½" side over the stabilizer and press. If the fold will not stay in place, consider using a strip of fusible web to hold the fabric firmly in place. Fold ½" over on the opposite side to enclose the raw edge and press. Fold the excess over the back of the strip and pin. Press. The entire back of the strip should be covered.

10. Topstitch the long edges of the strip, catching the folded edge on the wrong side. Set aside.

Closure Tab

1. Place the 4" x 17" strip of brown canvas, right side down, on a pressing surface.

2. Cut a strip of Stitch N Shape fusible stabilizer 1½" x 14". Place the stabilizer strip, glue side down, on the 4" x 17" strip of brown canvas as shown below.

2"

17"

1"

½" 2"

Fuse the stabilizer to the fabric. Flip the fabric over and press from the right side. This will make an indentation of the stabilizer, making it easy to locate the edges of the stabilizer strip.

3. Place the templates on the strip, evenly spacing the designs within the edges of the stabilizer. Slide a target sticker under each template. Remove the templates, one at a time, and write the design number on the target sticker. Repeat until the entire strip is full, leaving 1½" blank at one end and 4" blank at the opposite end. The stabilizer will extend 2" beyond the embroidery at one end and ¾" beyond the embroidery at the opposite end. The sample has five designs.

4. Hoop the fused fabric and polymesh stabilizer in the largest (longest!) hoop available. Attach the hoop to the machine and center the needle over the cross hairs of the first target sticker. If your machine has the trace feature, use it now to ensure the design is centered within the stabilizer area of the strip. Embroider the first design. Position the needle over the next cross hairs, remove the target sticker, and complete the design. Repeat for each design. Rehoop as necessary, repeating the steps above until all five designs are stitched.

5. Trim the excess polymesh stabilizer.

6. Place the embroidered strip right side down on a pressing surface. On the end that has 1½" blank, fold the raw edge (¾" seam allowance) over to the wrong side of the strip. Press. If the fold will not stay in place, consider using a strip of fusible web to hold the fabric firmly in place.

7. On the opposite end, fold the raw edge (2" seam allowance) over to the wrong side of the strip.

8. Press. Fold the ½" excess fabric on the long side over the stabilizer and press. If the fold will not stay in place, consider using a strip of fusible web to hold the fabric firmly in place.

9. Fold ½" over on the opposite side to enclose the raw edge and press. Fold the excess over the back of the strip and pin. Press. The entire back and all raw edges of the strip should be covered.

10. Topstitch the long edges of the strip, catching the folded edge on the wrong side. Set aside.

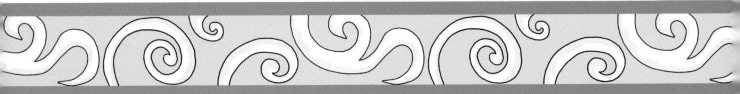

Decorative Patches

1. Hoop tear-away stabilizer and attach the hoop to the machine. Select design MEA4. Stitch the first color sequence, the placement guide. Place a 4" square of brown fabric over the design area, making sure the fabric completely covers the placement guide. Stitch the second color, the tack down.

2. Carefully remove the hoop from the machine but DON'T remove the fabric from the hoop. Trim the excess appliqué fabric. Reattach the hoop to the machine and finish the design. Remove the hoop from the machine.

3. Carefully tear off the excess stabilizer. Trim any whiskers from the edge of the embroidery designs.

4. Pin one patch to one end of the 36" embroidered strap, right sides up. Make sure the square end of the strip is hidden by the wide portion of the patch. Top-stitch into the satin stitching of the patch with monofilament thread, anchoring the patch to the strap. Repeat for the opposite end. Set aside.

Assemble

1. Sew the front facing to the front lining with a ½" seam allowance. Sew the back facing to the back lining with a ½" seam allowance

2. Sew the lining front to the lining back at the side seams. Sew the bottom seam leaving a 4" opening. Press all seam allowances open.

3. To form the purse bottom, match the side seam to the bottom seam at each side and pin. Sew. Set aside.

4. Make the loop for the tab closure. Cut a 3" x 1" strip of brown fabric. Fold the strip in half and press (3" x ½"). Fold under the raw ends (¼") and press. Pin the loop to the center of the front of the bag. Topstitch the ends of the loop to the bag. Set aside.

5. Pin the 2" blank end of the tab strip (1½" x 15") to the center of the back of the bag, extending the strip towards the top of the bag.

6. Topstitch the strip to the bag with monofilament thread.

7. Pin the front of the bag to the back of the bag, right sides together.

8. Sew the side seams and press the seam allowances open.

9. Insert a 4.0 twin needle. Topstitch the side seams, centering the seam under the machine foot.

10. Replace the twin needle with a regular needle. Sew the bottom seam. With right sides together, match the side seam to the bottom seam at each side and pin. Sew.

11. Turn the lining wrong side out. Insert the bag into the lining, matching the side seams. Pin the upper edge, keeping the closure strap away from the seam. Sew with ½" seam allowance. Turn the bag right side out through the opening in the lining. Sew the opening closed.

12. Press the top edge of the bag. Stitch ½" from the edge with a topstitching needle.

13. Center the shoulder strap on the bag side seam, positioning the bottom of the strap 5½" below the top of the bag.

14. Topstitch the strap to the bag, stitching through the strap, the bag, and the lining. Repeat for the other side seam.

Try Wearing With...

*Linen jacket,
full-leg linen trousers,
square-toe piped flats*

Alternate Color Idea

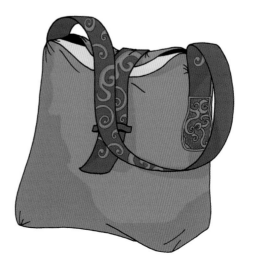

Swirly Slouch Belt

Decorative belt buckles have been around for years, but embroidered belt buckles are something new. With the advent of strong adhesive products, embroidered fabrics (or just embroidery designs) stay put—right where you place them. An embroidered belt buckle can become the focal point of a whole ensemble or just blend with an outfit—it's your choice.

Belts that snap open to accommodate different buckles are fairly easy to find. Available in shopping mall kiosks and leather stores, buy them in a variety of colors to complete your wardrobe. You'll find the blank buckles in sewing and leather supply catalogs. And the stitching is fast—just one design! Try different fabrics, designs, and decorative trims. The buckles are inexpensive so you can create different looks for the same belt.

Materials

❋ Oval belt buckle
❋ MEA20 design
❋ Red liner tape
❋ Polymesh stabilizer
❋ faux suede (6" x 8" piece)
❋ tracing paper

Embroider

1. Hoop polymesh stabilizer and green faux suede. Attach the hoop to the machine and embroider the MEA20 design.

Assemble

1. Make a pattern of the inner perimeter of the belt buckle by laying tracing paper over the buckle and tracing the inside. Cut out the pattern.

2. Center the pattern over the embroidery design and trace. Cut out the embroidery design.

3. Lay the pattern on a sheet of red liner tape and trace. Cut out the tape. Remove the protective paper and press the adhesive surface to the belt buckle. Remove the remaining sheet of paper. Center the embroidery design over the buckle and smooth the fabric as it adheres to the red liner tape.

What To Do if The Design is Not a Perfect Fit:

1. *If the fabric is too large for the belt buckle and extends over the metal border, use a box cutter or X-ACTO knife to trim the fabric. Just push the blade against the metal border and slice away the excess fabric.*

2. *If the fabric is too small and there are gaps between the fabric and the metal border, add some trim or bling! The trim should be very narrow and just sit inside the metal frame. Select a trim that doesn't ravel as the ends will have to remain unfinished. Bling is a terrific filler! Just add a row of metal studs or crystals around the inside of the metal border. Any gaps between the border and fabric will fade away when bling is introduced.*

Try Wearing With...

Jeans,
t-shirt,
clogs

Matte jersey dress,
chunky silver necklace on
leather rope,
silver dangly earrings,
cocktail ring,
dressy slingback
high heels

Alternate Color Idea

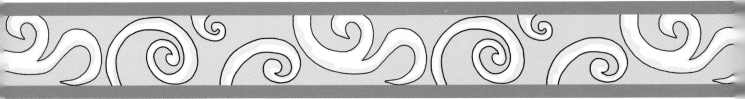

Town and Country Bag

The Town and Country bag conjures images of Audrey Hepburn. The classic combo of black and white is stunning, while the floral appliqués lend a touch of femininity. The narrow ribbon at the top (with a very ladylike bow) balances the expanse of embroidery at the base of the bag. But you don't have to stick with black and white—try red and blue; brown and beige; or pink and green or...just try something, you'll love it!

The Town and Country bag features more of my functional embroidery technique. This time the embroidery actually shapes the bag. There is no pattern for the bag; the beautiful curves are created by the appliqué designs stitched on each corner. You'll start with a plain rectangle of fabric and finish with a stylish handbag. The corner designs feature basting lines that will help you hoop squarely. You'll be toting the Town and Country bag in no time.

Materials

* ½ yd. white canvas
* ¼ yd. black canvas
* ⅓ yd. lining fabric
* 1 yd. of 1" wide decorative ribbon
* Magnetic clasp
* Polymesh stabilizer
* Scraps of Stitch N Shape Double fusible stabilizer
* Decorative purse handle (sample is 14")
* Magna-Hoop with the large rectangle frame
* Tracing paper or transparency
* MEA18 and MEA19 templates

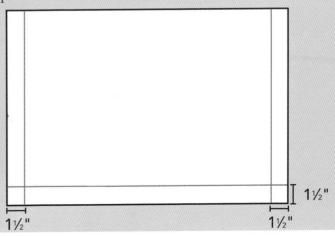

Cut

* Cut two 15" x 10" pieces of white canvas.
* Cut a 3" x 29" strip of black canvas for the gusset.
* From the lining fabric, cut two 13" x 9" pieces and one 3" x 29" piece.

* Using a quilter's ruler, chalk three lines, 1½" from the right, bottom and left sides of the front section as illustrated. Repeat for the back section.

1½"

1½"   1½"

Embroider

1. The corner design, MEA19, features a line of basting stitches that will help you position the corner designs perfectly square and perfectly reversed in the mirror image. Place the MEA19 template on the lower right corner of the fabric, positioning the design's basting lines on the chalked lines. Slide a target sticker under the template, aligning the cross hairs, and remove the template.

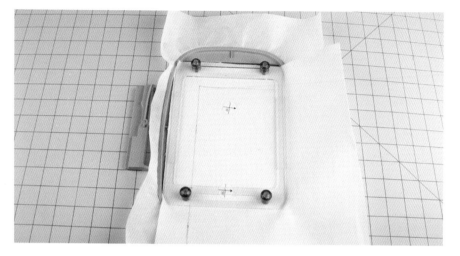

2. Hoop tear-away stabilizer. Insert the Magna-Hoop's metal frame. Lay the fabric in the hoop. Place the Magna-Hoop's large rectangular acrylic frame in the hoop. Position the fabric so that the chalked lines are inside and parallel to the edges of the opening. Snap the magnets into place.

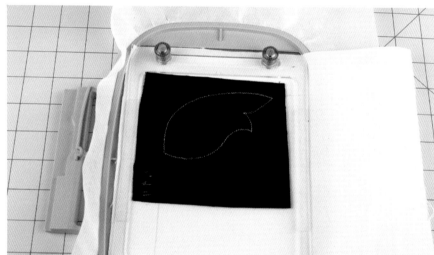

3. Attach the hoop to the machine. Position the needle over the target sticker and remove the target sticker. Sew the first color, the basting lines. Sew the second color, the appliqué placement guide. Cover the placement guide with a 4" x 4" scrap of black canvas fabric. Stitch the third color, the tackdown. Carefully remove the hoop from the machine but DO NOT remove the fabric from the hoop. Trim the excess appliqué fabric

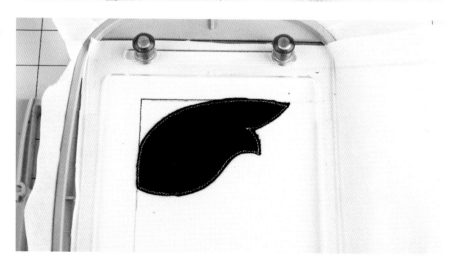

4. Reattach the hoop to the machine and finish the design.

5. Remove the fabric from the hoop. Release the fabric from the tear-away stabilizer and lay the fabric on a flat surface. Flip the MEA19 template over to position the design in mirror image. Place the mirror-imaged template on the left corner of the bag. Align the basting lines with the chalked lines. Slide a target sticker under the template, aligning the cross hairs, and remove the template.

6. In the editing screen on the embroidery machine, mirror image the design.

7. Hoop tear-away stabilizer and position the left corner of the bag in the Magna-Hoop as in Step 2. Complete the appliqué design.

8. Remove the bag from the hoop and from the tear-away stabilizer. Find the center of the bag by measuring the distance between the outer edges of the embroidered designs or by folding the bag in half, matching the corners. Mark the center at the chalked line. Place the MEA18 template on the bag—sit the template's cross hairs on the bag center, and place the lower edge of the design on the chalked line. Slide a target sticker under the template and remove the template.

9. Hoop tear-away stabilizer. Insert the metal frame of Magna-Hoop. Lay the fabric in the hoop. Place the Magna-Hoop large rectangular acrylic frame in the hoop. Position the fabric so that the chalked line is inside and parallel to the edge of the opening. Snap the magnets into place.

10. Attach the hoop to the machine. Position the needle over the target sticker and remove the target sticker. Sew the first color, the appliqué placement guide. Cover the placement guide with a 4" x 4" scrap of black canvas fabric. Stitch the second color, the tackdown. Carefully remove the hoop from the machine, but DO NOT remove the fabric from the hoop. Trim the excess appliqué fabric. Reattach the hoop to the machine and finish the design.

11. Repeat all steps for the back of the bag.

Assemble

1. On the wrong sides of the bag's front and back sections, place a ruler at a 45-degree angle on each embroidered corner. Chalk the point where the line touches the edge of the embroidery.

2. Trim the bag sections—leaving a ½" seam allowance around all the embroidery designs.

3. Place one trimmed section on top of both 13" x 9" pieces of lining. Trim the lining to the same size as the embroidered bag section.

4. Pin the front of the bag to the gusset, right sides together, with ½" seam allowance, easing the gusset around the corner curves. Sew the seam with the front of the bag up, facing you. Stitch with ½" seam allowance, stitching right into the embroidered appliqué.

5. Lay the front of the bag, right side up, on a flat surface. Place a pin on the gusset opposite each corner.

6. Pin the back of the bag to the gusset, matching the corners to the pins with right sides together. Sew with ½" seam allowance.

7. Repeat for the lining, leaving an opening for turning.

8. Place the bag on a flat surface. Mark a line 3" from and parallel to the top of the bag around the entire bag. Center the ribbon on the line and pin it in place. Topstitch the ribbon to the bag.

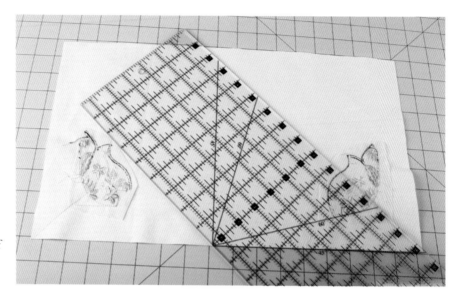

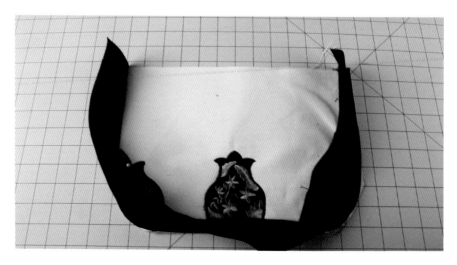

9. Cut a 10" length of ribbon and fold the ends into the center to make a 5" bow. Baste the ends in place. Fold a 2" length of ribbon around the center of the bow, hiding all ribbon ends. Baste to secure. Center the bow on the top-stitched ribbon and whipstitch in place.

10"

5"

10. Loop one 5" length of 1½" wide webbing through one purse-handle ring. Pin to the upper edge of the bag at the gusset, aligning the raw edges. Baste. Loop the remaining 5" length of 1½" wide webbing through the other ring. Pin and baste to the opposite gusset.

11. Turn the lining wrong side out. Insert the bag into the lining, right sides together, matching the gussets. Pin the upper edge. Sew with ½" seam allowance.

12. Turn the bag, right side out, through the opening in the lining. Sew the lining opening closed. Edgestitch the top of the bag.

13. Apply the handles following the manufacturer's directions.

Try Wearing With...

White cotton capris,
Black blouse,
gold cuff bracelet,
gold hoop earrings

Alternate Color Idea

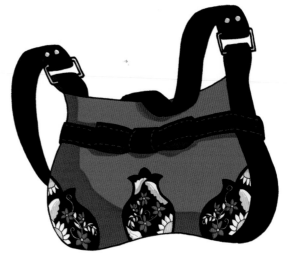

Town and Country Belt

Ever make a custom belt? You'll love the fit and the color and the embroidery, because, well, you designed it. A bit of stiffness is added by inserting belt backing or webbing into the embroidered tube. You can control just how rigid you want your belt—think comfort here and choose wisely. Take your time in selecting the fabric and thread, because you'll wear this belt for a very long time.

Follow the instructions for the Swirly Slouch belt on page 44 to create the belt buckle. Use design MEA20 to duplicate the sample shown here.

Materials

* Black faux suede (5" strip x waist measurement plus 8")
* Polymesh stabilizer
* Belt backing or belt webbing (1½" strip x waist measurement plus 6")
* Belt buckle
* Awl or eyelet cutter
* MEA17 design and three MEA17 templates
* Temporary spray adhesive
* Fasturn

54

Prepare

1. Measure your waist or hip and add 8" to the amount. Use that measurement to cut the faux suede.

2. Place a piece of tape, 4½" from one end and 2" from the opposite end. Write "Buckle" on the tape that is 2" from the end.

Embroider

1. Center the MEA17 templates on the width of the faux suede strip starting at the "buckle" tape mark. Place the edge of the first embroidery design on the tape. Evenly space the remaining templates about ¼" apart. Slide a target sticker under each template and remove the templates.

2. Hoop polymesh stabilizer in the largest hoop available. Spray the stabilizer with temporary adhesive. Finger press the faux leather into the hoop. Pin the faux suede to the stabilizer for added support.

3. Attach the hoop to the machine and position the needle over the first target sticker. Embroider the designs.

4. Remove the faux suede from the hoop and lay it right side up on a flat surface.

5. Place the edge of a quilter's ruler on the outside edge of the embroidery, extending the length of the ruler into the next area to be embroidered. Place the templates along the edge of the ruler, evenly spacing them as in the first group of embroidered designs. This will help you place and stitch the embroidery in a straight line. Slide target stickers under the templates and remove the templates.

6. Hoop polymesh stabilizer and the faux suede, centering the target stickers. Continue embroidering the designs as in Step 3. Repeat until the belt is completely embroidered, reaching as close as possible to the tape.

7. Remove the tape, but first note which end is the buckle end.

Assemble

1. Trim all excess stabilizer and thread tails.

2. Use a quilter's ruler to trim the strip to a 4" width, centering the embroidery in the strip. Fold the strip in half length-wise, right sides together, and sew the long edge with a ½" seam allowance.

3. Carefully center the seam allowance in the strip, and press the seam allowance open using a protective pressing sheet.

4. Turn the tube, right side out, using a Fasturn.

5. Slide the belt backing or webbing into the tube.

6. Center the seam on the back of the belt and press.

7. Fold in the raw edges on each end and pin.

8. Topstitch the ends shut.

9. Slide the buckle end of the belt onto the buckle ring.

10. Topstitch through all layers of the belt to secure the buckle to the belt.

11. Try on the belt and mark the hole(s) for the point of the buckle.

12. Use an awl or eyelet cutter to cut the hole.

Try Wearing With...

White cotton pique sheath, sunglasses, black pearl beaded necklace and earrings

Alternate Color Idea

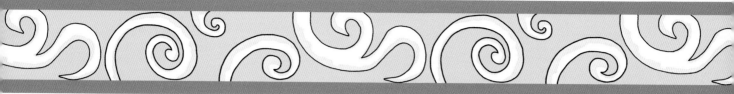

Chapter 3 Avant-Garde!

Secrets to Success

✳ Purchase a plain handbag in a shape and size you love, and then dress it up with dimensional flowers.

✳ Splurge on colorful accents when creating bags, belts, and shoes. A splash of colorful accessories updates even the most mundane wardrobe.

✳ Combine different fabrics to create more visual interest. Add contrast at the flap, corner patches, or gusset.

✳ Extend purchased straps by sewing strips of leather between the bag and handle, turning a purse handle into a shoulder strap.

✳ Plan the center medallion so that it accents the curve of the flap on a saddlebag. Hide the magnetic snap underneath (on the wrong side) of the flap.

Handles

Handle Attachment

Fabric

Appliqué Design

3-Dimensional Garden Party Straw Bag

The Garden Party Straw Bag is the easiest project in the book, so if you're looking for a quick fix, this is it. Use any bag; add contrasting but complementary faux suede flowers and you're off.

Stitch multiple repeats of the flower in one hooping by loading as many flowers as possible in the hoop. If you'd like, do this in software first, then color sort the flowers so it stitches quickly with few color changes.

Materials
* Straw handbag
* faux suede in turquoise (6" x 6"), beige (6" x 6"), and brown (8" x 10")
* Water-soluble stabilizer
* MEA9
* Red liner tape

Prepare

1. Open MEA9 in your embroidery editing software. Select the first color and delete it.

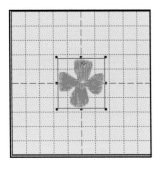

2. Select a 4" x 4" hoop. Load five repeats of MEA9 into the hoop, spacing the designs about 1" apart.

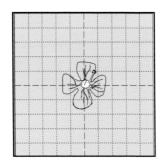

3. Save the design as MEA9Beige. Open a new file and select a medium-size hoop. Load 12 repeats of MEA9, again spacing them about 1" apart.

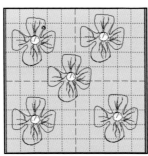

4. Save the design as MEA9Brown. Send both designs to the machine in the appropriate format.

Embroider

1. Hoop water-soluble stabilizer and turquoise faux suede in a 4" x 4" hoop. Embroider MEA9Beige, stitching colors 1 and 3 in dark brown and color 2 in beige. Remove the hoop from the machine and the fabric from the hoop. Set aside the embroidered fabric.

2. Hoop water-soluble stabilizer and beige faux suede in a 4" x 4" hoop. Embroider MEA9Beige, stitching colors 1 and 3 in dark brown and color 2 in turquoise. Remove the hoop from the machine and the fabric from the hoop. Set aside the embroidered fabric.

3. Hoop water-soluble stabilizer and brown faux suede in a medium hoop. Embroider MEA9Brown, stitching color 1 in dark brown and colors 2 and 3 in turquoise. Remove the hoop from the machine and the fabric from the hoop.

4. Tear away the excess stabilizer from the faux suede pieces. Cut out all the flowers, trimming very close to the stitched outline.

Adorn

1. Audition the flowers on the bag. I played with a few layouts before settling on an all-over pattern.

2. Once you're satisfied with the layout, attach each flower to the bag with double-sided adhesive tape. Leave the flowers on the bag as you tape each one down.

Try Wearing With...

Swimsuit with sarong, straw hat, sunscreen, sunglasses

Alternate Color Idea

Cheyenne Bag

Select upholstery-weight faux suede to give body to this dainty bag. Otherwise, fuse interfacing to the wrong side of the suede to add strength to a shapeless fabric. Consider a playful lining—like a shot of turquoise or hot pink.

The swirls and dots that decorate the corner patches and center medallion stand out when stitched in contrasting colors. For a more subtle look, try tone-on-tone, just make sure you don't match the thread fabric so perfectly that the embroidery fades into the background. After all, if you invest the time in creating the embroidery, you might as well see it.

Materials

* ¼ yd. brown faux suede
* ⅓ yd. lining fabric
* Magnetic clasp
* Polymesh stabilizer
* Scraps of Stitch N Shape Double fusible stabilizer
* Decorative purse handle (sample is 14")
* Protective pressing sheet
* Magna-Hoop with large rectangle frame
* Tracing paper or transparency for MEA1 and MEA2 templates
* MEA1 and MEA2 embroidery designs

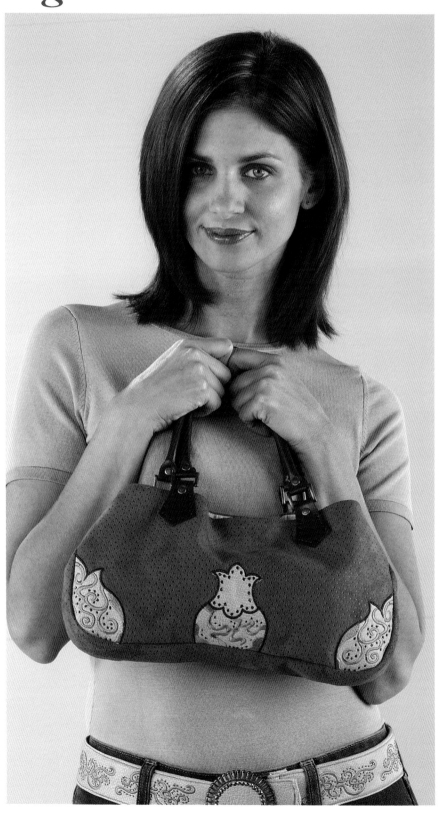

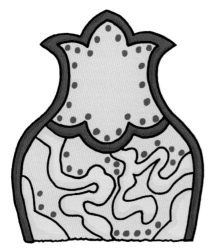

Prepare

1. Cut two 16" x 9" pieces and one 26" x 2½" piece of brown faux suede. Cut two 13" x 7½" pieces and one 26" x 2½" piece of lining fabric.

2. Using a quilter's ruler, chalk three lines, 1½" from the right, bottom, and left sides of the front section as illustrated. Repeat for the back of the bag.

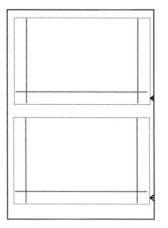

Embroider

1. The corner design, MEA1, features a line of basting stitches that will help you position the corner designs perfectly square and perfectly mirror imaged. Place the MEA1 template on the lower right corner of the fabric, positioning the design's basting lines on the chalked lines. Slide a target sticker under the template, aligning the cross hairs, and remove the template.

2. Hoop tear-away stabilizer. Insert the metal frame of the Magna-Hoop. Lay the fabric in the hoop. Place the Magna-Hoop's large rectangular acrylic frame in the hoop. Move the fabric, if necessary, so that the chalked lines are inside and parallel to the edges of the opening. Snap the magnets into place.

3. Attach the hoop to the machine. Position the needle over the target sticker and remove the target sticker. Sew the first color, the basting lines. Sew the second color, the appliqué placement guide. Cover the placement guide with a 4" x 4" scrap of tan vinyl. Stitch the third color, the tackdown. Carefully remove the hoop from the machine but DO NOT remove the fabric from the hoop. Trim the excess appliqué fabric. Reattach the hoop to the machine and finish the design.

4. Remove the fabric from the hoop. Release the fabric from the tear-away stabilizer and lay the fabric on a flat surface. Flip the MEA1 template over to position the design in mirror image. Place the mirror-imaged template on the left corner of the bag. Align the basting lines with the chalked lines. Slide a target sticker under the template, aligning the cross hairs, and remove the template.

5. In the editing screen on the embroidery machine, mirror image the design.

6. Hoop tear-away stabilizer and position the bag's left corner in the Magna-Hoop as in Step 2. Complete the appliqué design.

7. Remove the bag from the hoop and from the tear-away stabilizer. Find the center of the bag by measuring the distance between the outer edges of the embroidered designs or by folding the bag in half, matching the corners. Mark the center at the chalked line. Place the MEA2 template on the bag—sit the template's cross hairs on the bag center and the lower edge of the design on the chalked line. Slide a target sticker under the template and remove the template.

8. Hoop tear-away stabilizer. Insert the metal frame of the Magna-Hoop. Lay the fabric in the hoop. Place the Magna-Hoop's large rectangular acrylic frame in the hoop. Shift the fabric, if necessary, so that the chalked line is inside and parallel to the edge of the opening. Snap the magnets into place.

9. Attach the hoop to the machine. Position the needle over the target sticker and remove the target sticker. Sew the first color, the appliqué placement guide. Cover the placement guide with a 4" x 4" scrap of tan vinyl. Stitch the second color, the tackdown. Carefully remove the hoop from the machine but DO NOT remove the fabric from the hoop. Trim the excess appliqué fabric. Reattach the hoop to the machine and finish the design.

10. Repeat all steps for the back of the bag.

Assemble

1. On the wrong side of the bag's front and back sections, place a ruler at a 45-degree angle on each embroidered corner. Chalk the point where the line touches the edge of the embroidery.

2. Trim the bag sections—leaving ½" seam allowance around all the embroidery designs.

3. Place one trimmed section on one 13" x 7½" piece of lining. Trim the lining to the same size as the embroidered bag section. Repeat for the remaining 13" x 7½" piece of lining.

4. Pin the front of the bag to the gusset, right sides together, with ½" seam allowance, easing the gusset around the corner curves. Sew the seam with the front of the bag up, facing you. Stitch with ½" seam allowance, stitching right into the embroidered appliqué.

5. Lay the front of the bag, right side up, on a flat surface. Place a pin on the gusset opposite each corner. Pin the back of the bag to the gusset, matching the corners to the pins with the right sides together. Sew with ½" seam allowance.

6. Repeat for the lining, leaving an opening for turning.

7. Mark the position for the magnetic snap, 2½" down from the center of the top of the lining, front and back. Fuse a scrap of Stitch N Shape Double fusible stabilizer to this area on both the front and back lining. Apply the magnetic snap to the lining front and back (see instructions on page 16).

8. Turn the lining wrong side out. Insert the bag into the lining, right sides together, matching the gussets. Pin the upper edge. Sew with ½" seam allowance. Turn the bag, right side out, through the opening in the lining. Sew the lining opening closed.

9. Press the top of the bag.

10. Using a topstitch needle, topstitch around the top of the bag, ½" from the edge.

11. Use a large paper clip or binder clip to hold the handles in place. Topstitch the handles through all layers of the bag.

The faux-leather handle stitching lines are pre-punched by the manufacturer. Select a stitch length that matches the distance between the pre-punched holes. Thread the needle with a 30-weight rayon thread and carefully guide the needle into each hole. Sew twice to ensure durability.

Try Wearing With...

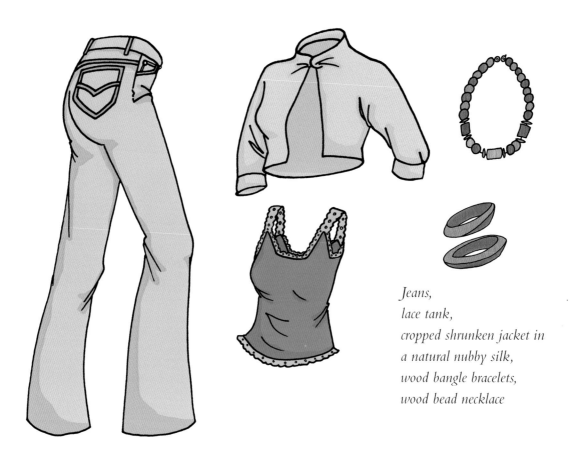

Jeans,
lace tank,
cropped shrunken jacket in
a natural nubby silk,
wood bangle bracelets,
wood bead necklace

Alternate Color Idea

Avant-Garde Bag

This boho bag will become a wardrobe staple—it's just the right size, has a magnetic closure, and sports a shoulder strap. I love the contrasting faux leather pieces—they really show off the embroidery and mimic the natural flecks, nicks, and grain of real leather. This bag, when created with "tough" fabrics, will carry you through the daily grunge of life. Throw it in the car, drop it on the kitchen table, sling it over your shoulder—it'll withstand it all. The flap and magnetic closure safely protects all your valuables as you get on with your busy life.

Materials

* ½ yd. dark brown faux leather
* ¼ yd. tan faux leather
* ⅓ yd. lining fabric
* Magnetic clasp
* Polymesh stabilizer
* Scraps of Stitch N Shape Double fusible stabilizer
* Decorative purse handle (sample is 14")
* Protective pressing sheet
* Magna-Hoop with the large rectangle frame
* Tracing paper or transparency for MEA5 and MEA6 templates

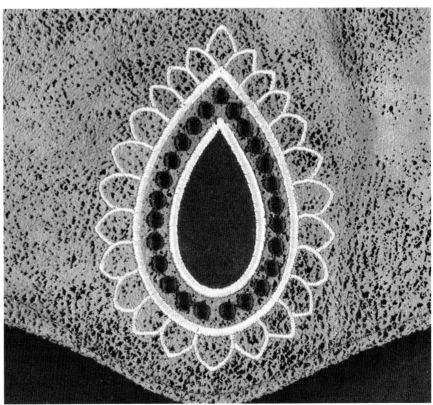

Prepare

1. From the dark brown faux leather, cut two 15" x 11" pieces; two 10" x 2" strips for the handle tabs; and one 3" x 28" gusset. From the tan faux leather, cut two flap sections from the pattern on page 127. From the lining fabric, cut two 12" x 9" rectangles and one 3" x 28" gusset.

2. Using a quilter's ruler, chalk three lines 1½" from the right, bottom, and left sides of the front of the bag as illustrated. Repeat for the back section.

Embroider

1. Place the MEA6 template on one of the lower corners on the Avant-garde front section. Align the edge of the MEA6 template with the drawn line. Slide a target sticker under the template and remove the template. Flip the template over for a mirror image of the original design and place it on the opposite corner. Slide a target sticker under the template, aligning the cross hairs. Remove the template. Repeat for the back of the bag.

2. Hoop polymesh stabilizer and insert the Magna-Hoop metal frame into the hoop. Position one design area (a corner) in the center of the hoop. Place the Magna-Hoop large rectangle frame on top of the fabric. Slide the magnets into the slots. Attach the hoop to the machine.

3. Position the needle over the center of the target sticker and remove the target sticker. Stitch the first color segment, the placement guide. Place a piece of tan faux

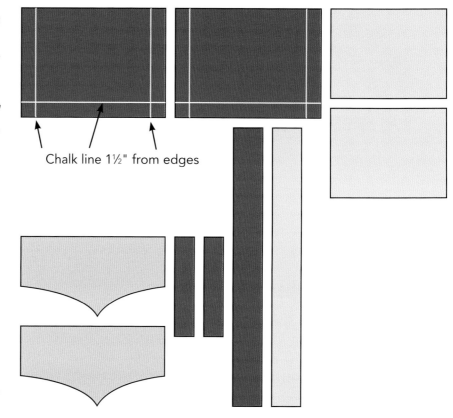

Chalk line 1½" from edges

leather over the appliqué area. Stitch the second color segment, the tack down. Carefully remove the hoop from the machine but DO NOT remove the fabric from the hoop. Trim the appliqué fabric close to the stitching. Place the hoop back on the machine and finish the design.

4. Repeat for the remaining three corners, mirror imaging the design when necessary.

5. Cut out the bag's front and back, adding a ½" seam allowance. Trim ½" outside chalk lines. The trimmed pieces should measure 9½" x 12".

6. Center the MEA5 template on the bag flap. Leave at least 1" around the lower section of the embroidery design. Slide a target sticker under the template, aligning the cross hairs. Remove the template.

7. Hoop polymesh stabilizer and insert the Magna-Hoop metal frame into the hoop. Position the point of the flap in the center of the hoop. Place the Magna-Hoop square frame on top of the fabric. Slide the magnets into the slots.

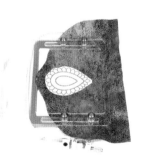

8. Attach the hoop to the machine. Position the needle over the target sticker and remove the target sticker. Stitch the first color segment, the placement guide. Place a piece of dark brown faux leather over the appliqué area. Stitch the second color segment, the tack down. Carefully remove the hoop from the machine but DO NOT remove the fabric from the hoop.

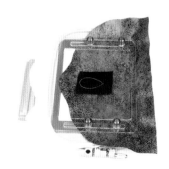

73

9. Trim the appliqué fabric close to the stitching.

10. Place the hoop back on the machine and finish the design.

Assemble

1. Sew the gusset to the bag's front and back, right sides together. Press all seams using a protective pressing sheet to avoid burning the faux leather.

2. To make the handle straps, fold ½" on each long side of the 10" x 2" strips. Edgestitch the strips. Slide one ring of the purse handle onto each strip. Baste the ends. Pin the strips to the upper edge of the gusset. Baste.

3. Sew the lining front and back, right sides together, to the gusset lining, leaving a 4" opening in one seam.

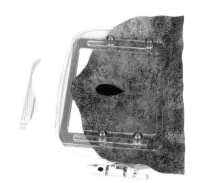
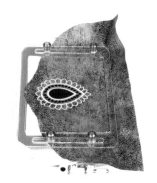

4. Place the flap and flap lining right sides together. Mark the center of the embroidery on the wrong side of the flap lining to locate the position of the magnetic snap. Fuse a scrap of Stitch N Shape Double fusible stabilizer to this area. Apply one half of the magnetic snap. Pin the flap to the flap lining, right sides together.

5. Sew the flap to the flap lining with ½" seam allowance. Trim and clip all curves. Turn right side out and smooth all seams with a point turner. Press with a protective pressing sheet. Edgestitch the flap.

6. Pin the flap to the back of the bag, right sides together. Baste at the upper edge. Flip the flap over the bag and mark the landing spot of the magnetic snap. Apply the other half of the magnetic snap to the bag as completed for the flap.

7. Place the bag, right side out, into the lining. Sew the upper edge with ½" seam allowance. Turn the bag right side out through the opening in the lining. Sew the opening closed. Edgestitch the upper edge of the bag.

Try Wearing With...

 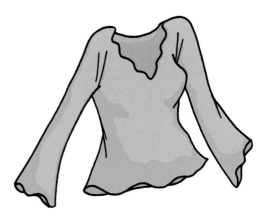

Jean skirt,
boho top,
big hoop earrings,
multiple strands of beads

Alternate Color Idea

Avant-Garde Belt

Add a dose of glam to a plain tunic and pair it with jeans or dress down a traditional sheath with this funky pieced belt. Use interesting hardware—I found 2½" silver rings but you might like copper, gold, or black. Or skip the rings and just embroider a long strip of leather (like the Town and Country Belt). Forgo embroidery on the belt buckle; let textured faux leather take center stage. Adjust the measurements of each section to fit your waist or hip. The instructions are for a finished belt measuring 42" including the buckle.

Materials

* ½ yd. dark brown faux leather
* Polymesh stabilizer
* Stitch N Shape Double fusible stabilizer
* Tracing paper or transparency for MEA8 template
* MEA8 embroidery design
* Two 2¼" silver rings
* Oval belt buckle
* Eyelet cutter or awl
* Magna-Hoop with medium rectangle frame
* Protective pressing sheet

Prepare

1. Cut the faux leather into three strips: one 17" x 4¼" (back section); one 12" x 4¼" (buckle section); and one 14½" x 4¼" (tab section).
Cut three strips of Stitch N Shape Double fusible stabilizer: one 13½" x 2" (back); one 8¼" x 2" (buckle section); and one 11½" x 2" (tab section).

2. In embroidery editing software, copy and paste MEA8 into a medium-size hoop (5" x 7"). A 5" x 7" hoop accommodates three repeats of MEA8. Mirror image one of the repeats and connect the three designs as shown. Make sure the designs connect. Save the design as LgBelt and print two templates on tracing paper.

3. Find the center of the 17" x 4¼" (back section) faux leather strip. Place one end of a LgBelt template at this mark. Turn over the second template to view the design in mirror image. Place it on the strip, connecting the first template with the mirror-imaged version. Use a ruler to help place the center of the templates in a straight line. Slide target stickers under both templates, aligning the cross hairs, and remove the templates.

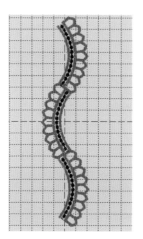

Embroider

1. Hoop polymesh stabilizer. Place the Magna-Hoop metal frame in the hoop. Position the faux leather on the metal frame. Place the medium acrylic frame on the faux leather and snap the magnets in the slots. Insert the template in the opening to make sure the design fits in the opening. Make any necessary adjustments. Embroider the first design. Remove the hoop from the machine. Remove the magnets and release the faux leather strip.

2. Hoop a new piece of polymesh stabilizer. Center the second target sticker in the hoop. Place the mirror-image LgBelt template back on the cross hairs. Make sure the image on the template connects with the stitched design. If not, make any necessary adjustments now. Secure the strip in the Magna-Hoop and stitch the design. Set the strip aside.

3. Measure 2" from one end of the 12" x 4¼" buckle section. Place one end of the LgBelt template at that mark. Adjust the template so that it sits in the center of the strip. Slide a target sticker under the template, aligning the cross hairs. Remove the template.

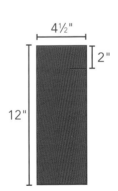

4. Hoop polymesh stabilizer and center the target sticker in the hoop. Place the Magna-Hoop metal frame in the hoop. Position the faux leather on the metal frame. Place the medium acrylic frame on the faux leather and snap the magnets in the slots. Embroider the design and remove the hoop from the machine. Remove the magnets and release the faux leather strip. Set aside.

5. Measure 2" from one end of the 14½" x 4¼" tab section. Place one end of the LgBelt template at that mark. Adjust the template so that it sits in the center of strip. Slide a target sticker under the template, aligning the cross hairs. Remove the template.

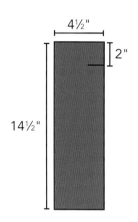

6. Hoop polymesh stabilizer and center the target sticker in the hoop. Place the Magna-Hoop metal frame in the hoop. Position the faux leather on the metal frame. Place the medium acrylic frame on the faux leather and snap the magnets in the slots. Embroider the design and remove the hoop from the machine. Remove the magnets and release the faux leather strip. Set aside.

7. Trim the polymesh stabilizer to within ¼" of the embroidery on all three strips.

8. Lay the embroidered strips on a pressing surface, right side down. Center the Stitch N Shape Double fusible stabilizer strips on the embroidered strips as shown. Fold one long edge over the Stitch N Shape. Place a pressing sheet over the belt section and press. Try to avoid placing the iron on the exposed Stitch N Shape. Fold over the second long edge and fuse.

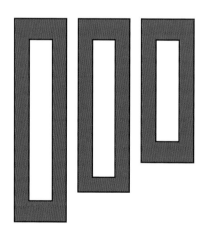

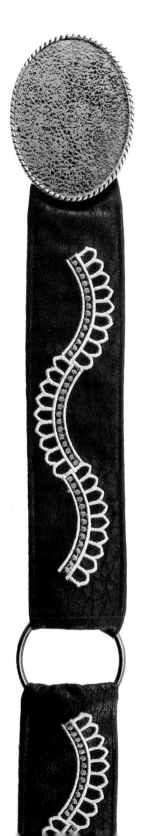

Assemble

1. Edgestitch both long sides of the belt sections.

2. Loop the rings through both ends of the back section. Pin the extra length to the embroidered section and sew to secure the rings.

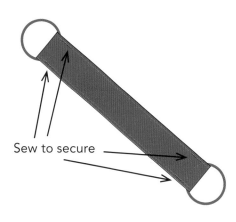

Sew to secure

3. Since the embroidery is not centered in the length of the buckle and tab sections, loop the shorter ends into the back section rings. The extra length on both sections (buckle and tab) allow for adjusting the length of the belt.

4. Try on the belt and make any necessary adjustments before attaching the buckle.

5. Place the tab end on a piece of wood and cut holes for the buckle with the eyelet cutter.

Try Wearing With...

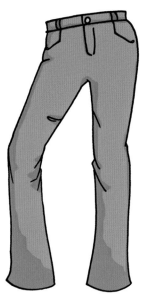

Jeans, turtleneck, suede shearling jacket, boots

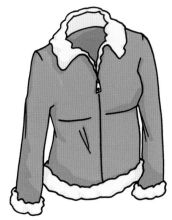

Alternate Color Idea

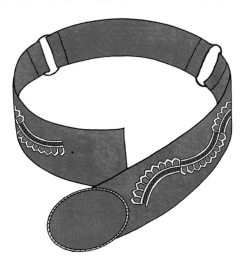

Avant-Garde Slides

I love this delicate lace that edges the shoe upper. I think it's a romantic touch to a mundane sandal. Just stitch on tulle and then attach it to the shoe. Don't nitpick on perfection. Remember, shoes are on the floor— far from critical eyes. Don't be concerned about trimming every fiber of the tulle or having a bit of leather show beyond the embroidery. If you've made a mistake, forgive yourself, make the best of it, and move on. Good lesson for life, too!

Materials
* ❋ One pair of mule sandals
* ❋ Tulle (8" x 10" piece)
* ❋ Water soluble stabilizer
* ❋ Red liner double-sided tape (¼" width)
* ❋ MEA14 embroidery design

Embroider

1. Hoop water-soluble stabilizer and two layers of tulle. Embroider four repeats of MEA14, rehooping as necessary.

2. Remove the tulle from the hoop and gently tear away the water soluble stabilizer. Trim the excess tulle as close to the embroidery as possible.

Adorn

1. Measure the edges of the shoe upper at the toe and at the instep.

2. Cut the red liner tape into two strips according to the measurements for the toe and instep. Peel the protective paper from the longer strips. Position the adhesive side at the edge of the instep. Smooth the tape onto the shoe, pressing the tape flat as it travels around the curve.

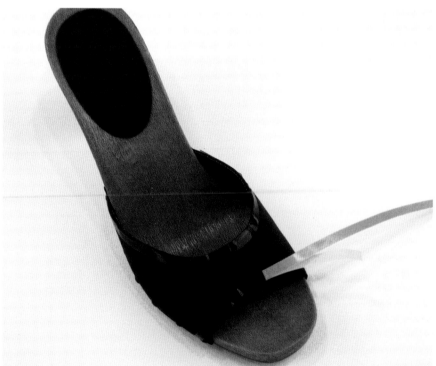

3. Remove the remaining protective paper from the tape. Place one end of the embroidered strip at one end of the tape and smooth the embroidery around the curve. Repeat for the toe edge and the other shoe.

Alternate Color Idea

Chapter 4 Footsy Fun

Secrets to Success

✻ Buy shoes that fit! There's no sense in decorating a shoe that brings you pain.
✻ Look for shoes with blank areas such as the upper on a mule, the heel on a wedge sandal, or the calf of a boot.
✻ Don't forget about house shoes—ladies love slippers. Velcro-closed terry cloth slippers are wonderful gifts and stitch up very quickly.
✻ Stitch the designs on tulle—they will be stronger and more durable during normal wear-and-tear.
✻ Think small—tiny embroideries go a long way on shoe embellishments.
✻ Position the double-sided tape on the shoe first, then finger press the embroidery design(s) to the sticky tape.

Slippers

Monograms on slippers, or any shoe for that matter, should read correctly for the person facing you—which is actually upside down if you're looking down at your feet. Always use a template and target sticker when hooping monogrammed items. It's easy to get confused as to "which way is up!"

Stitching on slippers looks difficult but these beauties snap open to reveal a flat flap. Use Magna-Hoop to hold the flap in the hoop. Or hoop sticky tear-away stabilizer, remove the protective paper, and finger press the flap to the hoop. Use a large hoop and embroider both slippers in one hooping (one at a time, of course!).

Materials

* Lettering software or font of your choice
* One pair of hook and-loop tape, side-closing slippers
* Tear-away stabilizer
* Water-soluble stabilizer
* MEA14 design and MEA14 template
* Magna-Hoop with square acrylic frame

Prepare

1. To determine the actual size of the design area on the flap, put the slipper on your foot and close the hook-and-loop tape. Measure the design area across the top of the foot, leaving an ample margin around the perimeter of the design so that it will not flow onto the edge of the slipper or too close to the insole. The design area on the sample measures 3" x 3".

2. Design MEA14 measures 61mm x 61mm (2½" x 2½"). Size the design to fit in the design area of your slipper. Save the edited design as MEA14b. Open MEA14b in embroidery software and merge a single letter into the center. Size the letter to fit inside the frame. Save the new design as MonoSlipper and send it to the embroidery machine in the appropriate format. Print a template of MonoSlipper.

Embroider

1. Center the template on the slipper upper. Slide a target sticker under the template, aligning the cross hairs. Remove the template.

2. Hoop tear-away stabilizer and insert the Magna-Hoop metal frame into the hoop. Open the slipper upper and center it on the hoop, laying the sole of the slipper away from the machine head. Place the Magna-Hoop square acrylic frame on the slipper. Snap the magnets into place.

3. Attach the hoop to the machine. Slide a piece of water-soluble stabilizer on top of the slipper and embroider the design. Remove the hoop from the machine and the slipper from the hoop.

4. Tear off the excess tear-away and water-soluble stabilizer. Dab any bits of remaining water-soluble stabilizer with a damp paper cloth.

5. Hoop a new piece of tear-away stabilizer and insert the metal Magna-Hoop frame. Place the second slipper on the hoop, positioning the sole away from the machine head. Rotate the design 180 degrees (do not mirror image the design when stitching a letter). Place the Magna-Hoop square acrylic frame on the slipper. Snap the magnets into place.

6. Attach the hoop to the machine. Slide a piece of water-soluble stabilizer on top of the slipper and embroider the design. Remove the hoop from the machine and the slipper from the hoop.

The acrylic frame may not lay flush on the hoop due to the bulk of the slipper. Engage the trace feature on the machine and watch the hoop as it travels through the design. If the slipper threatens to dislodge itself from the hoop, switch to a sticky stabilizer.

A Few Ideas for More Embellishment

✳   Glue a small ribbon bow to the outside of each
    slipper upper.

✳   Add hot-fix crystals to the monogram for more
    visual interest.

✳   Use red liner tape to outline the slipper upper
    with decorative trim, gimp, lace edging, or feathers!

Alternate Color Idea

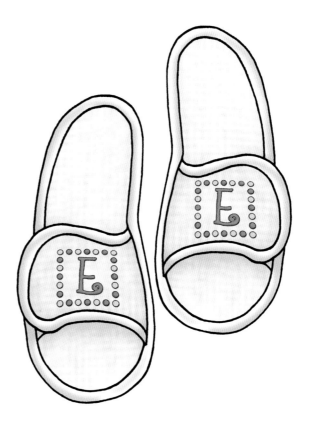

Town and Country Sandals

Dress up simple black slides with an embroidered patch of faux suede. So easy to do and simple to change, you'll love the versatility of this project. Shop for sandals with a three-part upper, like the sample. The narrow middle section is perfect for landing the embroidery and you won't have to worry about the edge where the shoe upper meets the sole. Use lightweight faux suede (dress weight) to reduce bulk. Match the suede to the leather sandal to help hide any imperfections in the final cutting and trimming.

Love the shoes so much you're worried about changing them? No fear, the Res-Q Tape is temporary so you can wear the sandals with embroidery or without!

Materials

* One pair of slide sandals
* Two 5" squares of black faux suede
* MEA16 design and one MEA16 template
* Tear-away stabilizer
* Magna-Hoop with narrow rectangle frame
* Res-Q Tape (¼" width)
* Scraps of muslin

Critique the Design

1. Place the MEA16 template on the sandal upper and ask yourself a few questions. Does the design fit? Is it centered? Is there a sufficient amount of space around the design or does it look crowded on the small upper? Tape the template to the shoe.

2. Try on the sandal with the template in place. Does the design look pleasing? You may see another necessary adjustment when the shoe is on your foot. If so, make the adjustments now in software and print a new template of the design.

3. Once you're satisfied with the design, save it in the appropriate format and send it to the machine.

Make a Muslin Template

1. Drape a scrap of muslin over the shoe upper and pin it in place. Determine the best way to cut the muslin to fit the upper. On the black sandal in the photograph, the muslin was cut at the edges to follow the curve of the leather. The rest of the fabric was wrapped under the upper and taped.

2. Carefully mark on the muslin where the fabric will be cut. Remove the muslin from the shoe and cut on the marked lines.

3. Place the muslin on the right side of a 5" square of faux suede and trace the muslin.

4. Flip the muslin over and place it on the other 5" square of faux suede. Trace the shape for the other shoe.

Embroider

1. Place the MEA16 template inside the traced shape on the faux suede. Slide a target sticker under the template and remove the template. Flip the template over and place it on the other piece of faux suede. Slide a target sticker under the template and remove the template.

2. Hoop tear-away stabilizer. Insert the Magna-Hoop metal frame. Place a 5" square of faux suede on the hoop. Place the narrow rectangle frame on top, shifting the fabric so that the target sticker is centered in the opening.

3. Attach the hoop to the machine, centering the needle over the target sticker. Remove the target sticker and embroider the design.

4. Remove the hoop from the machine and carefully dislodge the fabric from the tear-away stabilizer. Place the other 5" square of faux suede on the unused portion of the stabilizer. Place the narrow rectangle frame on top, shifting the fabric so that the target sticker is centered in the opening.

5. Attach the hoop to the machine, centering the needle over the target sticker. Remove the target sticker and embroider the design.

Adorn

1. Cut out the faux suede on the traced line.

2. Cut four short lengths (two for each shoe) of Res-Q Tape and re-move the protective paper from one side. Stick the tacky surface to the sandal upper at the sides, as close as possible to the leather edge. Just fold and crease the tape as needed to ac-commodate the curve. Repeat for the other shoe.

3. Cut four lengths (two for each shoe) of Res-Q Tape to fit the width of the shoe upper. Remove the pro-tective paper from one side and stick the tape to the underside of the shoe upper.

4. Remove the second layer of pro-tective paper from all strips of Res-Q Tape on one shoe.

5. Center the embroidered fabric on the upper and smooth it down, secur-ing it to the shoe with the tape.

6. Repeat for the other shoe.

Alternate Color Idea

Garden Party Sandals

Since it's impossible to hoop a shoe on a home embroidery machine, I'm always looking for creative ways to attach embroidery to shoes. A standard shoe clip is perfect for adornment at the center of the shoe upper. The clip has a flat side—where the embroidered design will be glued in place—and a hinge. The hinge slides under the shoe upper and grasps the leather. Try the clip on the shoe and wear the shoe for a few minutes. Pay attention to any discomfort—as you know, it will get worse with wear. I've found most clips are quite comfortable and completely unnoticeable. Shoes clips are an easy solution to adding dimensional embroidery to shoes. Just glue, tape, or hand tack the embroidery to the clip and Voila! Magic! Your plain janes are all jazzed up!

Materials

* One pair of sandals
* Brown faux suede (6" x 6")
* Water-soluble stabilizer
* MEA9 design
* One pair of shoe clips
* Double-sided adhesive tape

Prepare

1. Open MEA9 in your embroidery editing software. Select the first color and delete it. Select a 4" x 4" hoop. Load two repeats of MEA9 into the hoop that will accommodate all five repeats, spacing the designs about 1" apart. Save the design as MEAOutline.

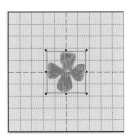

Embroider

1. Hoop water-soluble stabilizer and brown faux suede in a 4" x 4" hoop. Embroider MEA9Outline, stitching color 1 in dark brown, and colors 2 and 3 in turquoise. Remove the hoop from the machine, and remove the fabric from the hoop.

2. Tear away the excess stabilizer from the faux suede piece. Cut out the flowers, trimming very close to the stitched outline.

Adorn

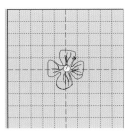

1. Place a small piece of double-sided adhesive tape onto the shoe clip. Finger press one of the flowers to the clip. Attach the clip to the shoe.

Alternate Color Idea

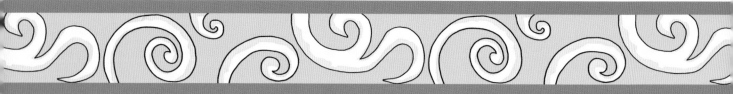

Chapter 5 Scarves and Such

Secrets to Success

* Focus the embroidery on a scarf near the ends to avoid scratchy threads around the neck.
* Use removable stabilizers on scarves since the wrong side of the embroidery is often visible.
* Consider using matching bobbin thread on scarves to make the embroidery reversible. Change the bobbin with every color change or match the bobbin thread to the scarf fabric.
* Afraid of stitching on beautiful velvet? Fear no more, flip it over and look at the wrong side of a velvet scarf. It's an ideal landing spot for a monogrammed pocket that's appliquéd in place.
* Combine fabrics and embroidery when decorating the large expanse of a garment bag. Adding contrasting pockets (big and small) is a quick way to transform a blank canvas.
* Avoid hooping unwieldy items by embroidering on flat fabric first, then sewing it to the item.
* Use decorative trim to link design areas together on a large item.
* Hold skinny belts securely in the hoop with Magna-Hoop.

Velvet Scarf

I found this scarf in a discount retail store and fell in love with the color. Knowing it was not a good candidate for embroidery because of the beaded trim, I purchased it anyway. Since it would be nearly impossible to add embroidery around the beads, I flipped it over and studied the wrong side of the scarf. Then it hit me—an embroidered pocket would be a luxurious personal touch. Now I use it to stash a lightweight item such as a credit card, room key, or cash.

Embroidering on velvet presents the same challenges as sewing on velvet—shifting fabric layers, lofty fibers, and a temperamental texture. One of the greatest concerns for embroidering on velvet is hoop burn. Magna-Hoop virtually eliminates hoop burn. The gentle hold of the acrylic frame does not mar the fabric and sliding a piece of tear-away stabilizer under the magnets erases any fear of pressure damage from the magnets.

Materials
* 6" x 8" piece of silk organza
* Velvet scarf
* Water-soluble stabilizer
* Size 75 metallic needle
* MEA13 design

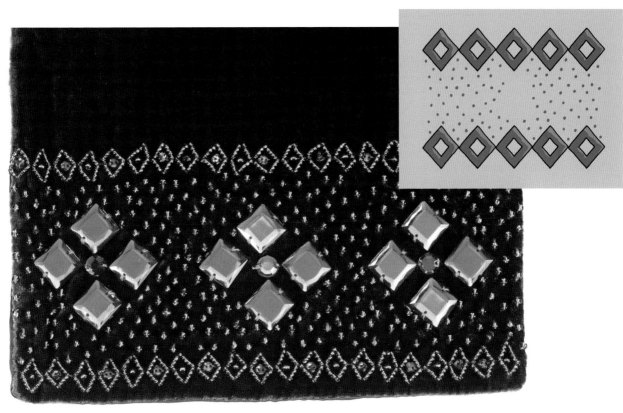

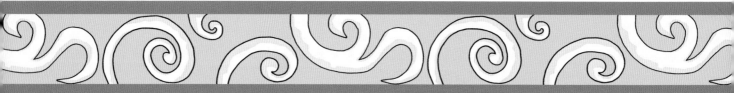

Prepare

1. Open MEA13 in embroidery software. Insert a single capital letter (first or last initial is appropriate) in the center of the design. Size the letter to 16mm x 24mm. Save the design as MEA13b and send it to your machine in the appropriate format.

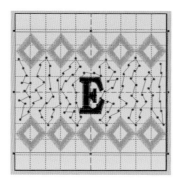

Embroider

1. Hoop water-soluble stabilizer and silk organza. Stitch MEA13.

2. Remove the fabric from the hoop.

3. Carefully tear off the water-soluble stabilizer.

4. Trim at the top and bottom edges as close to the embroidery stitches as possible.

5. Place the embroidered fabric on a pressing surface, wrong side up. Fold over the raw edges from both sides and press.

6. Trim away the excess fabric from the sides, leaving a ¼" seam allowance.

7. Pin the pocket to the scarf and sew the pocket to the scarf by hand. Do not sew the top edge.

Alternate Color Idea

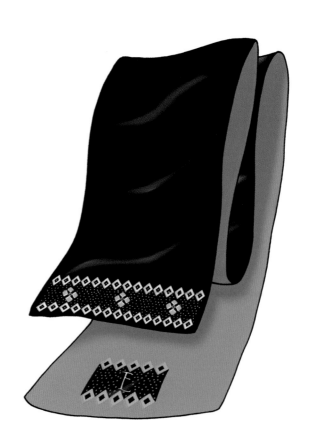

Try Wearing With...

Velvet blazer, jeans

Wool coat, gloves

Fleece Scarf

Dress up a plain, fleece scarf with an embroidered initial, decorative border, and a little bling! This is a great gift idea—one that you can repeat over and over again. Fleece is a fun fabric—casual, durable, and stretchy. Select designs that are a bit whimsical and free form. I've used a border and single-letter monogram, but falling leaves, snowflakes, or swirls and dots would work too. Search your stash for low-stitch count designs and experiment with the sporty nature of fleece. Below, I'll share my two favorite methods for embroidering on fleece. One technique uses the Magna-Hoop; the other technique uses a low-tack stabilizer.

Materials

* 6" x 8" piece of silk organza
* Fleece scarf
* Water-soluble stabilizer
* Size 75 metallic needle
* Tracing paper or transparency for MEA13 template
* MEA13 design
* Hot-fix applicator
* Metal studs
* Target stickers
* Magna-Hoop with large rectangular frame or self-adhesive, tear-away stabilizer
* Sulky Totally Stable tear-away stabilizer

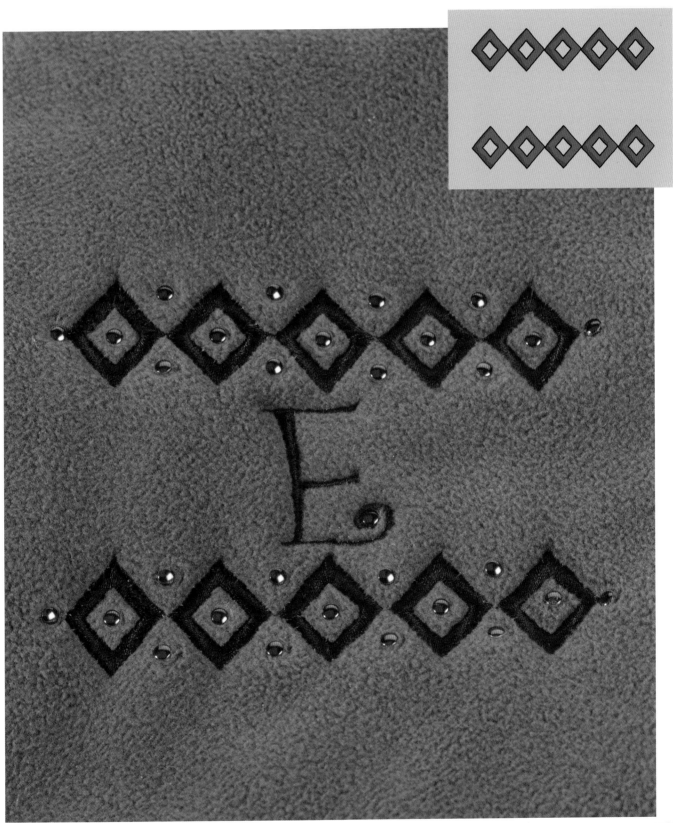

Prepare

1. Open MEA13 in your embroidery software. Delete color #2, the dots.

2. Insert a single capital letter (first or last initial is appropriate) in the center of the design. A whimsical or funky font is suitable for personalizing a casual fleece scarf, so select a font that fits the bill. Size the letter to 26mm x 30mm.

3. Place a transparency or tracing paper into the printer and print a template of the design. Save the design as MEA13L and send it to your machine in the appropriate format.

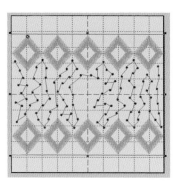

Embroider

1. Center the template on one end of the scarf, 3" from the end (excluding the fringe). Slide a target sticker under the template, aligning the cross hairs. Remove the template.

2. If the scarf is narrower than seven inches, Magna-Hoop is a great way to hoop the otherwise unwieldy fleece. Hoop water-soluble stabilizer and insert the Magna-Hoop metal frame. Lay the scarf over the frame, centering the design area in the hoop. Place the large rectangular frame on top and snap the magnets in place.

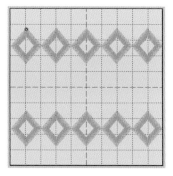

3. Attach the hoop to the machine and position the needle over the center of the target sticker. Remove the target sticker and place another piece of water-soluble stabilizer over the design area. Embroider the MEA13 design.

4. Remove the hoop from the machine and tear off the excess water-soluble stabilizer.

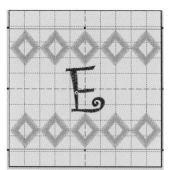

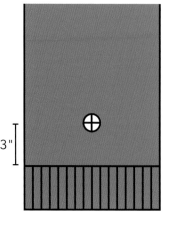

Add the Bling

1. Select a tip for your hot-fix applicator that fits the size of the metal studs. If the tip is much larger than the stud, there's a chance that the tip will actually burn or melt the fleece. Heat the applicator wand.

2. Place the scarf on a flat surface and audition the metal studs around the embroidery design. I opted to put a stud in each diamond and open area. I also added one stud to the foot of the E.

3. Once you're satisfied with the placement of the studs, touch the hot tip of the applicator to a stud and lift the stud off the fabric. Once the glue on the stud begins to bubble, set the applicator on the desired location and hold it in place for a few moments. Move to the next stud until all studs are glued.

Try Wearing With...

Chunky sweater, corduroy pants, warm boots

Alternate Color Idea

109

Garment Bag

Stylize a plain canvas garment bag, and it will never get lost in a sea of black luggage! The contrasting canvas, faux suede, and vinyl fabrics make the bag durable and rugged. And I'll show you how to add two pockets—one large pocket for shoes and one small pocket for tiny personal items.

Materials

* Canvas garment bag
* ½ yd. contrasting canvas
* 8" x 7" piece of faux leather
* 2½ yd. decorative faux leather trim
* 1⅓ yd. of faux leather binding
* Fabric glue or ¼" double-sided adhesive tape
* Satin stitch foot
* Tear-away stabilizer
* Embroidery editing software
* Lettering software or large letters built into the machine
* MEA10, MEA11, MEA12, and MEA22 embroidery designs

Simple Tips for Success

* ✳ Add all embroidery to flat fabric, then appliqué the embroidered panels onto the garment bag.
* ✳ Insert a quilter's ruler into the bag while pinning sections to the garment bag. The quilter's ruler will stop the pins from catching the other side of the garment bag.
* ✳ Unzip the bag and turn it wrong side out to sew the pockets and trim. Open the bag as wide as possible to access the design area. Working in this fashion allows you to sew on one layer of the garment.

Prepare

1. Measure the width of the garment bag and add 2". Measure the length of the garment bag and divide by three. This will be the height of the pocket. Use these measurements to cut the canvas, adding at least 3" on all sides to facilitate hooping. The pocket on the sample measures 23" x 12".

2. Divide the width of the pocket by three and mark the three separate sections with a quilter's ruler and chalk.

3. Fold the 6" x 7" piece of faux leather in half and in half again to find the center. Place a target sticker on the center of the right side.

At the Computer

1. If a large hoop or mega hoop is available, use it to embroider the large pocket. Open a new file in your embroidery editing software and select the largest hoop available. The sample was stitched in an 8" x 14" (160mm x 260mm) hoop. Open MEA 10, 11, and 12 and copy them into the new file. Starting in the upper left corner, space the design about 1" apart. Feel free to rotate the designs to add interest. Save the new file as Garment1.

2. Continue pasting the designs into the hoop in a logical path, saving your work as you proceed. Place the designs one next to the other so the needle will travel in a continuous path as the design sews.

3. Remove the color changes to stitch the design in one color, if desired.

4. Open MEA22. Copy and paste the small design into Garment1. Continue to sprinkle the design throughout Garment1. Save the design as Garment1 in the appropriate format.

5. Insert tracing paper or transparencies into the printer and print a template of Garment1.

6. Open lettering software and create a single letter monogram. The sample letter is 4½" x 3". Save the letter in the appropriate format and send it to the machine.

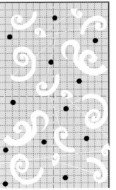

Embroider

1. When planning the embroidery layout of the large pocket, remember that faux leather trim will be stitched between each pocket section. Leave space between the repeats of Garment1 to accommodate the trim. Center the Garment1 template on one section of the pocket. Slide a target sticker under the template, aligning the cross hairs. Remove the template. Place the template on the next section and apply the target sticker. Repeat for the third section.

2. Hoop the pocket section and tearaway stabilizer. Position the needle over the target sticker and remove the target sticker. Embroider the Garment1 design. Remove the hoop from the machine.

3. Center and hoop the next pocket section with tear-away stabilizer. Position the needle over the target sticker and remove the target sticker. Embroider the Garment1 design. Remove the hoop from the machine and repeat the whole process for the remaining section.

4. Hoop the 6" x 7" piece of faux leather with tear-away stabilizer. Position the needle over the center of the target sticker. Remove the target sticker and embroider the single letter monogram.

5. Remove all excess stabilizer from the large and small pockets. Trim all thread tails.

Finish

1. Trim the large pocket to 24" x 13", this allows ½" on all sides to fold in the raw edges. Press the pocket from the wrong side, folding in ½" on all edges.

2. Sew the leather trim to the top edge of the pocket panel.

3. Pin the pocket to the garment bag. You might find it helpful to insert a large quilter's ruler into the garment bag to avoid pinning through all layers of the garment bag.

4. Turn the garment bag inside out and sew the pocket to the garment bag, topstitching close to the folded edge on the sides and bottom.

5. Run a bead of glue along the edge of the pocket panel or apply double-sided adhesive tape. Place the grommetted trim on top of the glue or tape.

6. Once dry, permanently sew the grommetted trim to the large pocket's outside edges using a wide, satin stitch foot. The open groove on the bottom of the foot will glide over the grommets. Center the foot right on top of the grommets, move the needle to the far right and stitch with a stitch length of 2.8 mm. Reposition the needle to the far left and sew down the other side of the grommets. Start and stop in the same position, always stitching in the same direction.

7. Turn the bag right side out and pin the monogrammed pocket to the garment bag. The pocket is centered 10" below the top of the bag. Turn the garment bag wrong side out and sew the monogrammed pocket to the top of the garment bag.

8. Turn the garment bag right side out and place it on a flat surface.

9. Use a quilter's ruler to chalk two lines from the monogrammed pocket to the large pocket, framing the small pocket.

10. Run a bead of glue on the chalked lines or apply double-sided adhesive tape. Place the grommetted trim on top of the glue.

11. Once dry, turn the bag wrong side out and permanently sew the grommetted trim to the garment bag as in Step 6.

12. Run a bead of glue along the bottom of the large pocket or apply double-sided adhesive tape. Place the grommetted trim on top of the glue.

13. Sew the leather trim to the bottom of the garment bag, covering the ends of the grommetted strips.

Alternate Color Idea

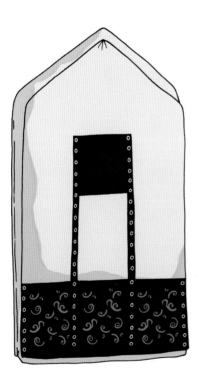

Try Wearing With...

Wrinkle-free brown rayon pants and top, clogs, a map, a passport

Vine Belt

Embroidering on leather and suede is challenging for home embroiderers. Look for a suede belt that is lightweight. If the leather is too thick and firm, the needle will not pass through the dense material. If it's possible to purchase two belts—one for testing and one for wearing—then by all means, buy two. Test the design on the test belt and keep that belt for future testing projects. The test belt might wind up looking funny, but no worries, you'll never have to wear it!

Design MEA21, created by Richards Jarden of EmbroideryArts, coordinates with his Romanesque collection. Richards designed this embroidery motif so that it would join seamlessly (no pun intended!). Just stitch one and place the next; it's so easy and so perfect! I love wearing this belt with the matching monogram. If these pants look familiar, maybe you remember them from my second book, Contemporary Machine-Embroidered Fashions (Krause Publications, 2006).

Materials
* Magna-Hoop
* Black tear-away stabilizer
* MEA21 design and three MEA21 templates
* Suede belt
* Needle

Embroider

1. Center the MEA21 template on the belt at the tab end as close to the first hole as possible. Slide a target sticker under the template.

2. Hoop black tear-away stabilizer. Insert the Magna-Hoop metal frame and place the belt on the hoop. Slide the Magna-Hoop medium acrylic frame on top of the belt. Shift the belt so that it is centered in the opening. Snap the magnets into the slots, securing the belt to the hoop.

3. Attach the hoop to the machine.

4. Center the needle over the target sticker. Engage the trace feature to make sure the design is centered in the width of the belt. Make any necessary adjustments with the jog keys on the machine.

5. Remove the target sticker and embroider the design.

6. Remove the hoop from the machine and carefully tear the belt off of the stabilizer, leaving as much stabilizer intact as possible.

7. Lay the belt on the opposite side of the hoop (on the unused portion of the stabilizer).

8. Place the Magna-Hoop medium acrylic frame on top of the belt, this time flipping it over to use the remaining stabilizer.

9. Continue embroidering the design until the entire belt is filled with embroidery.

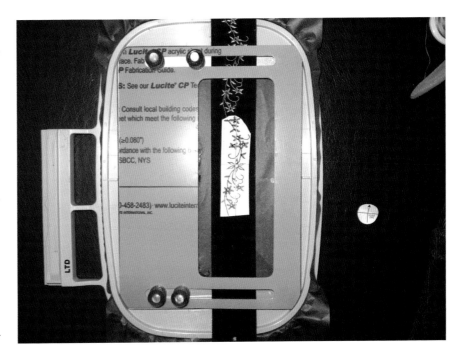

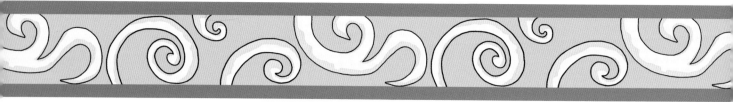

Try Wearing With...

*Corduroy pants,
long sleeve t-shirt, boots*

Alternate Color Idea

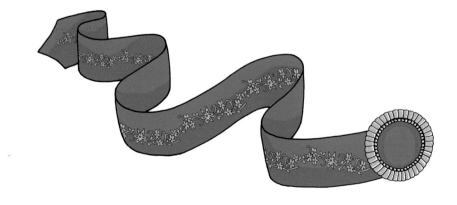

CD-ROM
Embroidery Designs

When you insert the CD-ROM into your computer, the menu may not appear on your screen automatically. To view the CD-ROM menu, click on the Start button on the lower left corner of your screen. Select My Computer. Then double click on Roche's Design CD. At this point, a menu will appear containing folders for each embroidery format: ART, DST, EXP, HUS, JEF, PCS, PES, SEW, SHV, XXX. Select the folder that corresponds to your machine brand.

MEA1

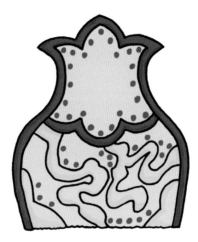

MEA2

MEA3

MEA4

MEA5

MEA6

MEA7

MEA8

MEA9

MEA10

MEA11

MEA12

MEA13

MEA14

MEA15

MEA16

MEA17

MEA18

MEA19

MEA20

MEA21

MEA22

MEA23

MEA24

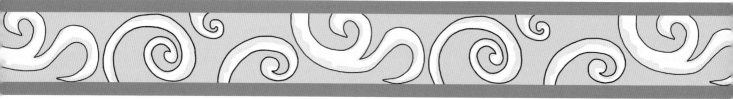

Embroidery Designs Color Sequences

MEA1
1. *Placement guide: brown*
2. *Tackdown: brown*
3. *Teal*
4. *Russet Brown*
5. *Brown*

MEA2
1. *Placement guide: brown*
2. *Tackdown: brown*
3. *Teal*
4. *Russet Brown*
5. *Brown*

MEA3
1. *Placement guide: brown*
2. *Tackdown: brown*
3. *Teal*
4. *Russet Brown*
5. *Brown*

MEA4
1. *Placement guide: brown*
2. *Tackdown: brown*
3. *Tackdown zigzag: brown*
4. *Teal*
5. *Russet Brown*
6. *Brown*

MEA5
1. *Placement inner oval: brown*
2. *Tackdown inner oval: brown*
3. *Placement outer oval: brown*
4. *Tackdown outer oval: brown*
5. *Brown*
6. *Beige*

MEA6
1. *Placement guide: brown*
2. *Tackdown: brown*
3. *Brown*
4. *Beige*

MEA7
1. *Brown*
2. *Brown*
3. *Beige*
4. *Black*

MEA8
1. *Brown*
2. *Brown*
3. *Beige*
4. *Black*

MEA9
1. *Pink*
2. *Dark pink*
3. *Yellow*
4. *Black*

MEA10
1. *Beige*

MEA11
1. *Beige*

MEA12
1. *Beige*

MEA13
1. *Silver*
2. *Gold*

MEA14
1. *Blue*
2. *Green*

MEA15
1. *Green*

MEA16
1. *Green*
2. *Blue*
3. *Yellow*

MEA17
1. *Green*
2. *Blue*
3. *Yellow*

MEA18
1. *Placement guide: Black*
2. *Tackdown: Black*
3. *Green*
4. *Yellow*
5. *Marigold*
6. *Blue*
7. *Orange*
8. *Black*

MEA19
1. *Placement guide: Black*
2. *Tackdown: Black*
3. *Green*
4. *Blue*
5. *Yellow*
6. *Marigold*
7. *Orange*
8. *Black*

MEA20
1. *Oval outline (should match fabric)*
2. *Green*
3. *Blue*
4. *Yellow*
5. *Marigold*

MEA21
1. *Black*

MEA22
1. *Black*

MEA23
1. *Teal*
2. *Brown*

MEA24
1. *Teal*
2. *Brown*
3. *Oval outline (should match fabric)*

About the Author

Eileen Roche is the founder and editor of *Designs in Machine Embroidery* magazine and author of *Contemporary Machine-Embroidered Quilts* (Krause Publications, 2004) and *Contemporary Machine-Embroidered Fashions* (Krause Publications, 2004). She started the magazine in 1994 as a newsletter and has grown it into the industry's leading source of inspiration for the home embroidery enthusiast. A love of fabric, thread, and texture led Eileen to embroidery, where she was able to combine all three.

A frequent guest on PBS television shows *Sewing with Nancy* and the *Linda MacPhee Workshop*, Eileen has designed embroidery collections for Amazing Designs and *Designs in Machine Embroidery*. One of the world's foremost experts in machine embroidery, Eileen has taught at industry trade shows across the United States, reaching thousands of machine embroidery enthusiasts. Since Eileen embroiders just as much, if not more, than her reader, she has brought solutions to many problems embroiderers face. Eileen has created numerous tools for the home embroiderer and has a patent for the In The Hoop Angle Finder.

Designs in Machine Embroidery is a project-based magazine published six times a year. Editorial content includes machine-embroidered fashions, quilts, home décor, and crafts, plus tips and techniques on software, fabrics, stabilizers, and more. Visit www.dzgns.com for more information.

Resources

Digitizing Services
Internet Embroidery
www.internetemb.com

Blanks
Slippers
AllaboutBlanks
www.allaboutblanks.com

The Sewphisticated Stitcher
www.TheSewphisticatedStitcher.com

Purse Handles
Nancy's Notions
www.nancysnotions.com

Magnetic Closures
Ghee's
www.ghees.com

Oval belt buckle
Tandy Leather Company
www.tandy.com

Embroidery Designs
The Perfect Towel Kit
(For the funky font shown on page 106)
by Designs in Machine Embroidery
www.dzgns.com
1-888-739-0555

Adorable Ideas Designs
www.adorableideas.com

Amazing Designs
www.amazingdesigns.com

Bobbi Bullard
www.bullarddesigns.com

Cactus Punch
www.cactuspunch.com

Creative Design
www.creativedesignembroidery.com

Criswell
www.k-lace.com

Designs in Machine
  Embroidery
www.dzgns.com

Embroideryarts
www.embroideryarts.com

Embroidery Central
www.embroidery.com

Holley Berry Collections
www.holleyberry.com

Laura's Sewing Studio
www.laurassewingstudio.com

Martha Pullen
www.marthapullen.com

OESD
www.embroideryonline.com

Smart Needle Embroidery
  Collection
www.smartneedle.com

Stitchitize
www.stitchitize.com

Zundt Design
www.zundtdesign.com

Crystals, Beads and Embellishments
Design by Dawn
www.designbydawn.com

Sue's Sparklers
www.suessparklers.com

Bullard Designs
www.bullarddesigns.com/

Embroidery Machines
Baby Lock
www.babylock.com

Bernina
www.berninausa.com

Brother International
  Corporation
www.brothersews.com

Janome
www.janome.com

Pfaff
www.pfaffusa.com

Singer
www.singerco.com

Viking
www.husqvarnaviking.com

Software
Amazing Designs
www.amazingdesigns.com

Brother
www.brothersews.com

Bernina
www.berninausa.com

Baby Lock
www.babylock.com

Buzz Tools
www.buzztools.com

Designer's Gallery
www.designersgallerysoftware.com

Generations
www.generationsemb.com

Husqvarna/Viking
www.husqvarnaviking.com

OESD
www.embroideryonline.com

Origins
www.originssoftware.com

Pfaff
www.pfaffusa.com

Singer
www.singerco.com

Vikant
www.vikant-emb.com

Thread
Coats & Clark
www.coatsandclark.com

Madeira
www.madeirausa.com

Mettler
www.amefird.com/mettler.htm

Robison-Anton
www.robison-anton.com

Sulky
www.sulky.com

Stabilizers
Floriani Sewing and Quilting
  Products
www.rnkdistributing.com

Hoop-It-All
www.hoopitall.com

Madeira
www.madeirausa.com

OESD
www.embroideryonline.com

Sulky
www.sulky.com

Viking
www.husqvarnaviking.com

Embroidery Placement Tools
Designs in Machine Embroidery
www.dzgns.com
1-888-739-0555

Supplies
Nancy's Notions
www.nancysnotions.com

All About Blanks
www.allaboutblanks.com

The Sewphisticated Stitcher
www.sewphisticatedstitcher.com

Shoppers Rule
www.shoppersrule.com

Magazines
Designs in Machine Embroidery
(Editor Eileen Roche)
www.dzgns.com
1-888-739-0555

Sew Beautiful
www.marthapullen.com
1-800-547-4176

Sewing Savvy
www.clotildesewingsavvy.com

Sew News
www.sewnews.com
1-800-289-6397

Threads
Taunton Press
www.taunton.com/Threads/

Books
Krause Publications
www.krausebooks.com
1-800-258-0929

½" Seam Allowance

Swirly Slouch Bag

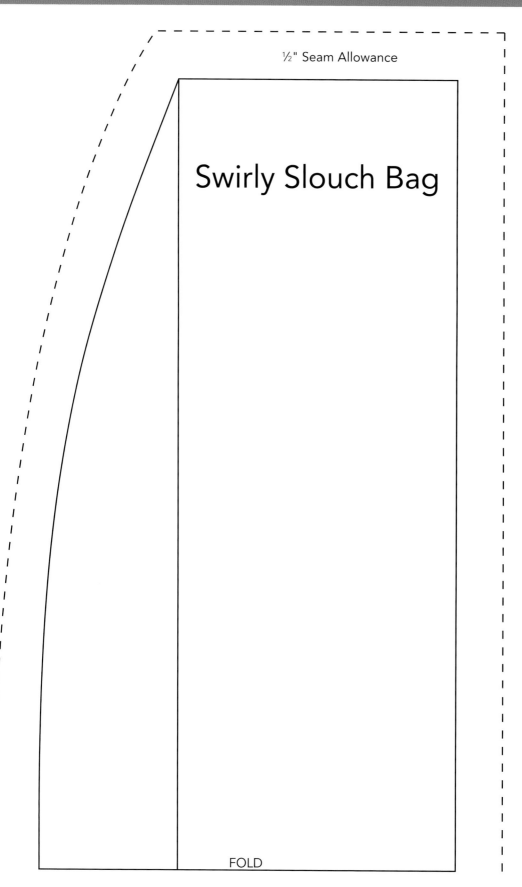

FOLD

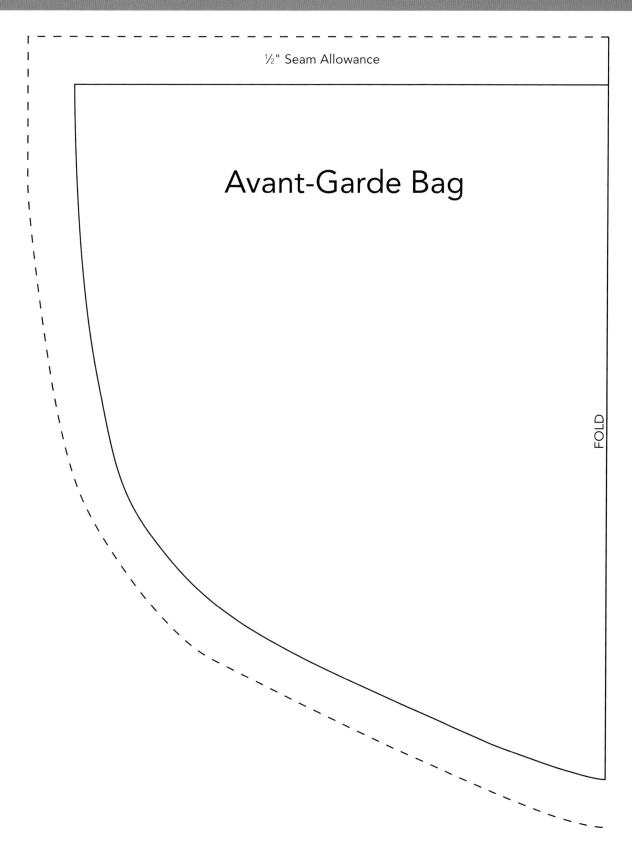

½" Seam Allowance

Avant-Garde Bag

FOLD

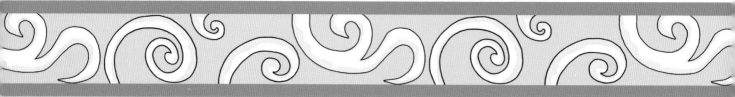

Turn Blanks into Brilliance

More Innovation from Eileen

Contemporary Machine-Embroidered Fashions

Transform Everyday Garments into Designer Originals

by Eileen Roche
Transform your wardrobe using machine embroidery to add stylish touches to 20 projects, including jeans, Capri pants and jackets, covered in 30 designs on an included CD-ROM.

Softcover • 8¼ x 10⅞ • 144 pages
125+ color photos and illus.
Item# MEFF • $29.99

Contemporary Machine Embroidered Quilts

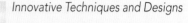

Innovative Techniques and Designs

by Eileen Roche
Moves from the basics of material selection and design, to twelve fabulous projects that combine quilting and embroidery. Patterns for quilts and embroidery designs are included on a free CD-ROM.

Softcover •8¼ x 10⅞ • 144 pages
75 color photos, 75 illus.
Item# MEQ • $27.99

Elegant Machine Quilting

Innovative Heirloom Quilting Using Any Sewing Machine

by Joanie Zeier Poole
Heirloom machine quilting can be done on a standard sewing machine. Incorporate the techniques into 20 simple projects such as napkins, table runners, wall hangings and coasters, featured in the full-size quilting patterns.

Softcover • 8¼ x 10⅞ • 144 pages
200 color photos and illus.
Item# ELMQ • $24.99

Machine Embroidery with Confidence

A Beginner's Guide

by Nancy Zieman
Nancy Zieman explains the basics of machine embroidery including what tools to use, how to organize the embroidery area, types of machines, designs, templating/positioning, software, stabilizers, trouble shooting and finishing touches.

Softcover • 8¼ x 10⅞ • 128 pages
100 color photos
Item# CFEM • $21.99

Fill in the Blanks with Machine Embroidery

by Rebecca Kemp Brent
Feed your need for more machine embroidery opportunities by exploring this unique guide, and its advice about blanks - where to find them, how to choose threads and stabilizers, and what techniques to use. Includes a free CD-ROM with 24 designs.

Softcover • 8¼ x 10⅞ • 48 pages
125 color photos
Item# Z0747 • $24.99